"*Reframe Your Story* is a life-altering book. If you're prone to fretting about all you're not doing and quickly dismissing all that you are (for your organization, your kids or yourself), you need this book. Tammy Heermann weaves together inspiring stories, compelling research findings and practical how-to steps into a compelling call to action."

LIANE DAVEY, *New York Times*–bestselling author
of *You First* and *The Good Fight*

"The single biggest limiting factor standing between you and the life you want is the story you are telling yourself. With *Reframe Your Story*, Tammy Heermann teaches you how to change your life. I saw myself in these pages, and you will too. Do not miss this book."

LAURA GASSNER OTTING, *Washington Post*–bestselling
author of *Limitless*

"An incredible resource for women at all stages of their careers and a must-read for anyone who coaches, leads or mentors women. With *Reframe Your Story*, Tammy Heermann has given us a generous gift— an accessible collection of insights powered by storytelling."

BETH WILSON, CEO, Dentons Canada LLP

"An essential read that helps women reframe the stories they tell themselves, stories that often hold them back and prevent them from achieving their full potential. *Reframe Your Story* is filled with insightful and relatable examples. Women can put Tammy Heermann's tools and tips into practice immediately to build their confidence and achieve their personal and professional goals."

ANNA FILIPOPOULOS, EVP and chief people and
culture officer, Four Seasons Hotels and Resorts

[Handwritten note:] Can you share with our listeners what imposter syndrome is, why men push through versus women letting it hold them back and what women can do to push through it. and how can taking risks help?

"Stories are powerful. In this encouraging book, Tammy Heermann shows us how to reframe our narratives so we feel better about our lives, and do what matters."

LAURA VANDERKAM, author of *168 Hours*
and *Juliet's School of Possibilities*

"The ultimate 'get it done' leadership book for badass women who want to take over the world. Actionable, insightful and ass-kicking, it won't just reframe your story, it will reframe your life!"

LESLIE EHM, *Wall Street Journal*–bestselling
author of *Swagger*

"A new expectation for leadership is emerging, and we need more talented women to step into the challenge. This book answers that call."

JIM REID, chief HR officer, Rogers Communications

(6) If we don't believe something is possible you suggest we check where that belief originates —> How would you suggest a listener do that?

(7) Instead of ducking the risks of stepping up, you suggest we focus on seizing the rewards, Tammy. What does that look like & what are some of the rewards we should consider?

(8) How can people tune in to catch their negative stories + how would they best reframe those stories?

(9) A recent study highlighted that women were less likely than men to know how they wanted their careers to advance and were less likely to have a vision for their future. This is where you recommend having a personal vision. Can you unpack that for us?

) For a long time, many believed that women suffered from an ambition gap, which isn't true, based on a BCG study. Can you share more on this one and the actual ~~causes~~ of the challenges women face at home and in the workplace.

) How do women's expectations of themselves hold them back relative to men and what do we need to be doing in the workplace to reduce the issue?

2) When it comes to learning, many women ~~have~~ a continuous learning mindset, but ~~the~~ challenge is it may not ~~be~~ well directed. This reminds me of conversations I have with my son about the difference ~~between~~ practice + deliberate practice that's meant to drive specific outcomes. Can you unpack this and how women can overcome this.

3) Many of us, Tammy, simply look forward to getting home and having a glass of wine or binge watching Netflix ——→, which isn't a satisfying way to live. How ~~can~~ we look up, and further out on the horizon and use purpose to improve this?

) How often would you suggest someone revisit their personal vision statement and what would you recommend as a process, rhythm + routine?

) I loved your line "From 'I get a shitload done' to 'I gotta do less shit'", can you unpack this?

) Research shows that one ~~area~~ women are behind men in leadership is strategic visioning and identified 3 reasons. You ~~both~~ have 3 common patterns that explain the tactical rut. Can you take us through this 1 at a time and how to overcome them?

REFRAME YOUR STORY

(16) a. The first, executing with excessive pride

b. second, having ed to too much work

c. third, making ourselves sub servient

(17) one of the biggest challenges for women in a meeting, Tammy, is they are afraid to sound stupid. When they do talk, they couch their uncertainty behind weakeni qualifiers → how can we overcome this?

(18) Two other challenges women face are fearing people won't like them and needing to be perfect. How do you work with women to overcome this?

Real Talk for Women

Who Want to Let Go, Do Less

and Be More—Together

(19) A challenge for many women is expecting their results to speak for themselves, whether its believing their results are self-evident; a fear that self-promotion is bragging; and, managers should just "know"... How do you work with your clients to address this, Tammy?

(20) You shared a great story about team dynamics and office politics as it relates to pre and post meetings and one of your workshop attendees, Celia. What are pre and post

TAMMY HEERMANN

REFRAME YOUR STORY

PAGE TWO

meetings and what did Celia learn?

1) An interesting study you wrote about illustrated that men tend to create networking relationships that provide multiple resources, such as friendship and relationship, which I recognize is true of everyone of my relationships, whereas, women don't like their worlds to collide. why is there such difference and how can women address it?

how can women overcome this need to be perfect!

22) If I've been talking to young women on my team about networking and they have a fear of doing it and feel "cross" leveraging their network, how do I help them overcome it and these two feelings and realize the value they can bring to others in a reciprocal way?

3) one of the biggest challenges I've seen for women in my life is the need to be perfect, which is worsened by social media, especially Pinterest + Instagram +

(24) Tammy, what else do you want to share with our audience today that we may not have covered?

Cataloguing in publication information is available from Library and Archives Canada.
ISBN 978-1-77458-116-2 (paperback)
ISBN 978-1-77458-117-9 (ebook)

Page Two
pagetwo.com

Edited by Amanda Lewis
Copyedited by Crissy Calhoun
Proofread by Alison Strobel
Cover design by Jennifer Lum
Cover illustration by Michelle Clement
Interior design by Fiona Lee

reframeyourstorybook.com

Ava, I hope you'll think this book's message is from the olden days. But in case you need it, here it is.

CONTENTS

INTRODUCTION
YOU NEED NEW STORIES

ONE DAY ABOUT five years ago, my family was setting out for a walk to the park. My daughter was seven at the time. Just as we started down the sidewalk, she reached out and grabbed my arm, pulling me backward.

"Mom, stop. Daddy has to walk first."

Confused, I asked her why.

"Because he's the leader," she said.

Even more confused, I asked her why her dad was the leader.

"Because he's a boy."

My heart sank. This from the child of a woman who has spent over a decade working to advance women's leadership. This from a girl whose father is a progressive feminist. My husband and I were both leaders in our workplaces and we split domestic duties. Everything I was fighting for, everything I thought possible for the future, was dashed in one phrase: *Because he's a boy*. What story was our daughter telling herself about her opportunities? I would soon find out what other stories were swirling around in her mind.

When she was eight, my daughter asked me in a fit of exasperation why we couldn't be a *normal* family. A perfect TV-normal family where the dad goes to work, and the mom stays home to walk the kid to school and volunteer for field trips. The fascinating thing is that the story she was telling herself was not the norm anymore. She was referring to the fact that I had a career. Not only is female workforce participation high, but in our immediate circle, every woman works outside the home. Many of those women closest to her—her aunts, her friends' moms, my girlfriends—not only work but are or have been the primary breadwinners.

When she was nine, my daughter came home from school on Equal Pay Day and asked me a series of questions about what she had learned. In her most incredulous voice, she asked how it was possible that a man and a woman could be paid differently for doing the exact same job. She went on to mock the situation, as only an elementary schooler can: "So yeah, like, here Mike, here's your dollar. And Sally, you get seventy-five cents." She stopped and looked at me, imploring, "Mom, that's so stupid. Why? How is that even possible?" I worried that her anger would subside and that, like so many women, she would grow up to unconsciously doubt her contribution, her monetary worth and whether she was doing enough to deserve more.

When she was ten, my daughter came home and asked an entirely different question. "Mom, why when a woman has a baby, does it automatically take the name of the dad, even when the mom has her own last name... and she's the one that *had* the thing? Sometimes the mom's name gets put in the middle, but no one ever says it. It's like it's not even there!"

She was already thinking about the roles of parents, about the pecking order in society and about her lasting impact. But would she remain steadfast in her conviction, ready to change the world like so many young girls when they start out? Or would she acquiesce and tell herself, *Well, that's how it is. What can I possibly do to change it?*

My daughter couldn't see beyond the current reality because she needed new stories. I bet you do too.

If you're like most women, from the moment you wake all your energy is put into making it through the day. Pick the right outfit, do your hair, execute your well-honed five-minute makeup routine, brush your teeth but be sure it's after you eat and have coffee and before you insert the Invisalign, but for god's sake don't drip on your clothes. If you take care of other life forms, there's the barking and screaming to abate, organize and get on their way. Exercise? Hmm, not today. By the time you start work, you're exhausted. You've lived your day by nine a.m.

You dive into endless emails, voicemails, pings, notifications, pop-ups, chats and knocks on the door. There's no time to breathe, let alone pee or nourish yourself. You scurry from one commitment to another as you constantly monitor yourself and your impact, trying to add value, make a difference, speak up, stand out, be passionate but not emotional, be decisive but not assertive. All the while, random worrisome thoughts interrupt your flow. *Did I sign the form? What's for dinner tonight? Is Cori's uniform clean? Did I pay the dog walker? Did I send a card for that birthday? Focus. Back to work. Did my team send that report yet? Can I get a few minutes with my boss to discuss that crisis? Have I checked with his admin?*

Somehow, it's the afternoon and you haven't eaten yet. You haven't even begun to tackle the crucial to-do list, and yet magically more urgent things have arisen to surpass yesterday's. And great, tomorrow you're supposed to attend a workshop for female leaders. You're supposed to talk about your aspirations and dreams and goals of rising up. As if. It would be nice, maybe, if you had the time. Right now, not a chance.

That's where I've met you, or women like you. I've met thousands of women over the past decade from around the world. I hear stories of exhaustion stemming from the responsibility for everything at home and at work. I hear the fury and the resentment of being overlooked, unheard and passed over. I hear story after story of heartache, heartbreak and heartburn. Amazing women like you have let me into your world by sharing your doubts, your regrets, your concerns, your pressures. I hear stories of single moms struggling, of breakdowns and burnout, of illness and tragedy, of toxic cultures and bosses, of abuse and danger. I hear your stories of exhaustion. I hear your stories of hopelessness. They are real.

I also hear other stories. Stories of hope and potential. Stories of taking on new roles and letting go of perfectionism and unrealistic expectations. Stories of promotion and pride. Stories of learning and mentorship. Stories of gaining control and possibility. But the sad reality is there's not enough of these stories. And there should be. There needs to be. There will be.

Why the stories you tell yourself are important

Stories are central to being human. They are the primary way we communicate at school, at work and around the dinner table. We read stories in books, we watch them on screens and we listen to them on podcasts, radios, around the boardroom and around the campfire. They are passed down from generation to generation and help shape our knowledge, beliefs and values. We love to hear a good story and we marvel at great storytellers, whether it's your CEO, your grandma or Steven Spielberg.

We know the power of story. We understand that stories can change us and others, and they can persuade. They can make us feel happy and hopeful, like *Toy Story* or *Forrest Gump*, or they can make us feel miserable and disappointed, like the series finale of *How I Met Your Mother* or *Game of Thrones*, depending on what you're into. Stories can boost bravery or feed fear. They can unite us or destroy us.

However, we rarely examine the most important stories: those we tell ourselves. We pay no attention to the vivid characters we have created in our own minds. Just like in a classic tale, there are villains and heroes, plot points and highs and lows. You tell yourself stories every day about your value, your worth, your capabilities and your skills, which taken together rival the best Agatha Christie novel. You create inner dialogues that match Margaret Atwood's or Jane Austen's. Shonda Rhimes would be envious of the intrigue, conspiracy and deception that live in your stories. Don't believe me? Think of the last fight you had with a friend, relative or partner. Ugh, I'm right, aren't I?

You have an internal narrative, a plot that continuously runs through your brain. Sometimes it's quiet and playing in the background and you barely know it's there (*La, la, la, I'm cruising through this meeting like it's nothing*). Sometimes it's loud and menacing, like when you're about to make that big presentation (*Who is going to listen to you? Literally WHO?*). This inner story shapes your sense of self: your beliefs about who you are and what you're capable of. Sometimes you draw on positive stories to help yourself get through, to build resilience and to muster courage to tackle the tough stuff. And sometimes you draw on and perpetuate the self-limiting stories, ruminating on times you've failed.

Why do these stories matter? The stories you tell yourself shape the behaviors in which you engage. If you tell yourself you are brave, that you can do it, that you've succeeded in the past, then you will try new things, apply for that job or have that tough conversation with your boss. When you reinforce your best self, you are more likely to try, strive and succeed. If you tell yourself you're not experienced enough, you don't know enough or that now is not the time, then you will behave in defeatist ways. You will stop yourself from attempting, from learning.

As Emily and Amelia Nagoski so aptly remind us in *Burnout: The Secret to Unlocking the Stress Cycle*, you will never completely erase these negative voices, so don't even try. It's more helpful to befriend your inner critic and thank it for the part it has played in keeping you safe. The trick is to say, "Thank you for trying to help, but now I'm going to trying something new."

Women who grow, excel and advance share commonalities in their mindsets. They tell themselves self-affirming stories for the most part, and when the inevitable self-defeating thoughts materialize, they use strategies to keep them at bay. Don't worry, I'll share the strategies with you too. These women also refuse to believe that there are limits on their success. There may have been factors all around them that could have prevented their success, but they didn't let those get in the way of their own beliefs in what they could accomplish. They tell themselves, their families and their organizations a story that is proud and not riddled with guilt. They don't believe the world is out to get them or that they have something to prove. If you're picturing someone giving the patriarchy the middle finger, that's what I'm picturing too.

Once you change the conversation you're having with yourself, then you can change the conversations you're having with others in order to achieve your personal and professional goals. Reframing your story means you can adjust your behaviors, exhibit new skills and transform perceptions others have about what you can accomplish. Yay, you!

The unhelpful stories we tell ourselves

This book is for you if you have doubted yourself or tried to be everything to everyone at all times. It's for you if you have questioned how you got here or marveled at how you got anywhere. It's for you if you have told yourself you don't know enough to speak out at that meeting, that you're not experienced enough to ask for that opportunity or don't have enough time to think about your next move, never mind what's for dinner.

I wrote this book for women. If you identify as a woman, then it is for you. Throughout the book, I draw on research that was conducted on women. It's safe to assume, however, that the term *women* in these studies was used to mean cisgender women, those who were assigned female at birth and identify as female. So much of this area of research also excludes nonbinary people, and as a cis woman I acknowledge my limitations in writing about the range of experiences outside my gender identity. I also acknowledge that there is no single universal experience of women and that various intersections of identities impact our experiences.

This book is for anyone who feels that they are constrained by forces larger than themselves and are looking for how to reframe their stories to break through those feelings. It's also for people (mostly cisgender men) who want to learn how it feels to operate in a world that for the most part is stacked against them. Women are still largely under-represented in management and leadership in corporations, government and society. Biases and stereotypes are rampant; old boys' clubs, glass ceilings and glass cliffs remain. There is much work to do here, requiring a persistent push for organizations, leaders, cultures and societies to evolve.

Many authors write books that address the ways women can become more effective or take charge of their destiny, while missing the bigger societal and cultural contexts that hold women back. A single mother working multiple jobs and struggling to put food on the table can't magically hire a nanny. The odds are low that a lone woman in an all-male department will win that promotion after her second maternity leave. These realities have caused a backlash to advice aimed at helping women feel more personally valued, more in control or more empowered.

One study looked at whether it was best to focus on structural issues or the tactical DIY strategies that women can implement themselves. The researchers found that those people who were exposed to the DIY messages were more likely to believe that women have the power to solve gender inequalities at work and, unfortunately, that they are also responsible for both causing the problem and fixing it.

First of all, I'm here to tell you that none of this is your fault. You are not here to be fixed nor are you solely responsible for fixing thousands of years of patriarchy. The unhelpful stories we tell ourselves are a product of the societal and cultural context we're in. But it still feels shitty to tell ourselves these stories and live with the implications of never keeping up, never getting ahead and never being treated equally or better than. And until we tell ourselves stories that make us feel strong and deserving, we cannot begin to challenge the structural barriers. So yes, there are countless systemic, legal, political, cultural and societal elements that need to change. I get it, I do. It's just not the focus of my writing here. If you want to read more about that, there are many awesome books out there on the structural issues.

In this book, I speak leader to (aspiring) leader by documenting a pattern of mindsets and behaviors I've observed in my work with women. For some of us, the stories we tell ourselves can be even more dangerous and limiting than the structural barriers we face. When we choose to tell ourselves stories that perpetuate feelings of not belonging, of subservience or low worth, we buy into the systemic issues we face. They promote and prolong the power of the dominant narrative. And let's face it, feeling powerless feels pretty crappy too.

Over a decade of leading women's development initiatives, I've found that women often stop themselves from growing, developing or advancing. Sometimes it's before they even come up against the external structural barriers. Sometimes they hold back from applying for a job because they don't believe they have enough experience, only to realize with anger later that the successful incumbent is less qualified than they are. Or they turn down a leadership opportunity that would pit them against the mostly male C-suite.

You control a lot more than you know. In this book, I'll shine a light on aspects of your life and career you can directly control. You control your thoughts, your mindset and your behaviors. You control where you choose to work and who you surround yourself with.

My goal is to help you reframe some of the stories you tell yourself that are not serving you. Imagine feeling lighter and more empowered. You have the opportunity; it's possible.

The story I tell myself

Who am I? I'm no one famous. This isn't a memoir of coming out on the other side of a grueling fight. I don't preach from a pulpit of a seven-figure salary. I'm not a doctor delving into your psyche. I'm like you. We haven't lived the same journey, but we've felt the same at times.

Over a decade ago, when I ran the leadership development practice at a consulting firm, our CEO came to me with a "project." A close contact of his was asking for help. His daughter was running a successful company that organized networking luncheons for women that featured inspirational speakers. But her aspiration was bigger. She didn't want to merely motivate women; she wanted to do something to actually increase the number of women in leadership roles. To do this, she needed a strong leadership development partner. She was looking for someone to create and run publicly offered workshops for women seeking to advance. "Make it work," I was told.

My company didn't offer public workshops. We created custom programs for organizations willing to pay a premium. This project entailed a whole lot of work for me and little money for my business. But I did it, and it opened up my whole world. I am still amazed that what started out as a pet project for me has grown into a passion. As a speaker and facilitator, I have been fortunate to reach thousands of women worldwide who have taken charge of their leadership careers. But more than that, I lived the leadership journey alongside these women. As I progressed from a senior consultant to a senior vice president, I found myself dealing with the same myriad challenges that these other women were facing.

I questioned myself, confronted self-confidence issues and endured criticism about my presence as a leader. I battled the introvert's plight of reflecting in, instead of speaking out, after being told by a senior leader that I took up a chair but it felt like I wasn't even there. I second-guessed my ability to be a good team leader, and I struggled to get out of the weeds to show I could be a strategic thinker and build a business. All the while, I was starting a family, experiencing secondary infertility and feeling immense guilt for not staying home when my daughter repeatedly asked why I had to work. I packed and unpacked suitcases on a weekly basis, becoming too comfortable in, and at the same time too choosy about, hotel rooms. I passed my child to a babysitter and passed my husband in the halls as we said hello and goodbye in the same breath. I struggled with what felt possible for my career, my health, my relationships, my happiness. Did it really have to feel this hard?

I then realized that I was making things way harder than they needed to be. While I couldn't control much of what was happening around me, I could change what I told myself. And once I told myself a different story, I felt more in control and my behaviors reflected that. Perceptions of my leadership changed. Upon examination, I realized I had many thoughts that were self-limiting, self-defeating and self-sabotaging. I had been working against myself. I needed to recognize and appreciate the positive aspects of myself, my work and my environment. I needed to reframe. That is what I did, that is what I continue to do for myself and for women like you, and that's what we're going to do in this book. Sound good?

How to reframe your stories

Your life and your career shouldn't be happening to you; you should be shaping them through your choices.

You deserve to feel strong, empowered and in control of your career choices. Maybe you want to rise to more senior levels of leadership, maybe you want to expand your current role by continuing to stretch, maybe you want to move into a new field. Maybe you want to stay put but carve out boundaries to focus on other important aspects of your life that are not getting enough attention. Your definition of success is your definition, not someone else's. Whatever your goals, the reframes in this book will make them feel possible for you.

Reframing is a common tool in psychology. It helps individuals see themselves or another person, relationship or situation in a different way. How you are in the world depends on the lens through which you view that world. Reframing is about shifting the lens and how you interpret what you experience. Take the camera on your phone, for instance. You can zoom in or out. You can focus on a portion of the object or include more content in the frame. You can apply a snappy filter to change the tone or mood or apply a sticker before you put it on Insta. You can literally reframe the picture to create a story for the viewer.

"Step out of the history that is holding you back. Step into the new story you are willing to create."

OPRAH WINFREY

That's what we need to do with the unhelpful stories we tell ourselves. We need to see them in a different light, change the color, add or remove content.

This book asks you to think about the unhelpful stories you tell yourself that may be holding you back. I outline seven of the most common stories that need to be reframed. Each chapter follows the same structure and begins with three unhelpful stories you likely tell yourself. They are the blockers in your brain, the barriers that prevent you from seeing another story, and they often result in behaviors that limit your success. Next, I provide a brief activity for you to further explore these stories. Then I outline the reframes—how to tell yourself new stories through your thoughts and behaviors.

Chapter 1, Believe It's Possible, begins with the biggest and most fundamental story: What do you tell yourself about your potential? Your answer determines your starting point—how you think about taking on something more, new or different. It will challenge you to redefine how you think about learning, experience and potential. Are you pigeon-holed in your job, level, organization or in your own skin? We'll examine the engrained misbeliefs that women don't belong or don't have what it takes to excel in roles with increased scope. This chapter is about seeing the possible.

Chapter 2, Look Up, Look Out, is about reframing your day-to-day from merely getting through to taking small steps toward your desired future. It examines the merits of not being on autopilot to the point that you are left wondering where the time went and how you got where you are. It makes the case for being purposeful about shaping the future you want with decisions and energy, which will build deliberately over time. Have you convinced yourself that you are successful only when you are using your well-honed skills and experience? Do you tell yourself that you'll think about your future when you have a little more time on your hands? This chapter will shift your perspective so that each day, even the hectic ones, you are creating momentum toward a personal vision. You will focus your attention on what matters most to you personally and professionally.

Chapter 3, Do Less Shit, delves into the stories we tell ourselves about being a good team player, pitching in and working hard to get it all done. Do you bask in being a fastidious firefighter or master multitasker? If so, it might be causing more harm than good. You'll go from getting shit done to making strategic decisions (i.e., doing less shit). Being strategic is about getting off the hamster wheel. It challenges you to question the value you add at work and home and what it's costing you. This chapter compels you to move from striking off tasks on long to-do lists to actioning strategic priorities, from constantly being busy to adding value. It will challenge you to change what you're known for so you can learn how to complete valuable tasks that matter to your brand, your earnings, your promotability and your health and well-being.

Chapter 4, Rule That Meeting, tackles the stories that determine how you show up during your daily conversations at work. Do you bite your tongue for fear of sounding stupid? Do you worry that if you voice your opinion, you won't be liked? Or do you face backlash when you do speak up? Do you search for the perfect way to say the perfect thing? This chapter focuses on meetings because that's where most of us spend a lot of our work time. A meeting can be a one-on-one conversation, a team gathering or a large group assembly. It can be formal or informal and with a variety of people. What I'm getting at is that there are multiple times a day where you can be impactful or invisible. If you're tired of clamming up, being shut down or striving for the perfect thing to say, then this chapter will reenergize you to show up and speak out for both your own benefit and for everyone on your team.

Chapter 5, Own It, Flaunt It, Get It, is about being proud of your accomplishments, your successes and your strengths. It reframes the story you tell yourself that engaging in this dialogue is selfish, that it's bragging or boasting. Instead, you'll learn to be a strong self-advocate, able to talk about your capabilities and ask for opportunities because of them. Do you believe that your results should speak for themselves, that if you put your head down and do great work that you'll be noticed, that someone will tap you on the shoulder for an exciting opportunity? If so, it's time to tell yourself a different story.

Chapter 6, Think *Who* before *Do*, looks at your belief that results matter more than relationships. Do you tell yourself you don't have time to network because you have real work to do? Do you believe that organizational politics is a colossal waste of time and everyone should just get over themselves and get back to work? This chapter will challenge how you think about building relationships for personal gain by reframing from smarmy to strategic. You will learn to value networks and organizational savvy alongside results and productivity. You will come away with a story that propels you to expand your network because it helps you do more of what you love, better and more quicky.

Chapter 7, Lighten Up, Brain, is about feeling buoyant, free and strong. Are you too hard on yourself? Do you attempt to live up to unrealistic expectations? Do you have difficulty letting things go? This chapter examines the stories you tell yourself over and over about guilt, perfection and striving to be all things to all people. You will be challenged to move from owning and controlling to letting go, from dripping in guilt to delighting in gratitude, and from ruminating to releasing. It *can* happen, and this chapter will show you why it's critical that it does.

1:1:1 Plan

Each chapter ends with what I call the 1:1:1 Plan. Because I believe so strongly in small but consistent steps, I've built a framework for you to apply learnings and practice new ways of thinking—once a week, once a month, once a year. What is the one thing you can do each week (or sometimes each day) to train your brain to tell yourself a different story? What is the one thing you can try each month to get out of the whirlwind and focus your energy and efforts on important priorities? What is the one thing you can think about yearly to reflect, celebrate and recalibrate?

Choose an activity that I've suggested or make up one of your own. I only ask that you pick a maximum of three concepts and really practice the heck out of them before moving on to another one and another one. Start small and see the power of accumulating small wins into big successes. See how you can slowly rewire your brain as you shift your default and change your stories.

People often give up on learning a new skill or perspective because it seems too daunting. I suggest you use the situations you are in multiple times a day as opportunities to practice new mindsets and behaviors. You likely have hundreds of interactions a day with yourself and with others in your workplace, your home or on the street. Use them. The more frustrating, the better. That way you practice new behaviors and new mindsets. You're busy, take the twofer.

For example, it's hard to muster up the courage to all of a sudden approach your boss and ask for a promotion. But if you slowly train your brain to believe in your value, to ask for what you want and let go of fears of what might happen if you do, then it doesn't seem so daunting after all. Build your strength in lower-risk situations before having a big conversation with your boss.

How to get the most out of this book

I ordered the chapters in this book to begin with the biggest stories, which verge on existential: *What do I believe is possible for myself? What is my horizon?* Then I move to more tactical stories: *How do I spend my time, speak up and get noticed?* While I hope you read each chapter, and in the order written, each chapter is discrete, and you can bounce around as you see fit. What's important is that you get out your pen, pencil, highlighter and stickies, or use the note functions on your e-reader. I designed this book so that you can engage with it: mark it up, put a question mark next to concepts you want to understand further, cross out positions you don't agree with, highlight tips you want to try, dog-ear a page you want to come back to.

Use the crap out of this book, then pass it on to someone who you think can benefit from it (or better yet, tell them to buy their own damn copy). Send me a note to tell me your stories, let me know what resonated and what didn't, and send me a photo of your well-worn copy. You can email me here: tammy@tammyheermann.com. Let's help each other and change our collective stories.

The power of sharing our inner stories

I told you the story of how my daughter believed that boys, not girls, were leaders. At the age of seven, she could not articulate why she believed what she did. But my questioning must have really stuck with her because, wouldn't you know it, two years later she explained why she believed Daddy was the leader.

We were in the living room after dinner and out of the blue she said, "Mom, you know why I said boys were leaders?" I nearly got whiplash with how quickly I turned my head. How could she have remembered after all this time?

She went on to recount a camping trip we had taken that year with a number of families. We took the kids on a hike over rocks and steep inclines. As we got to the first precarious spot, one of the dads told the kids to wait so he could go first, so he could help the kids, if necessary, get down the incline. One of the rambunctious boys then raced forward asserting, "I'm going next!" From this simple innocuous interaction, my daughter rationalized that boys always go first; boys lead. She likely reinforced the story that boys are leaders by making observations in the world around her over the next two years.

After she shared her explanation, we talked about what leadership really is and how it's not about gender at all. We talked about rambunctious behavior and quieter behavior and that both have their time and place, their advantages and disadvantages. We talked about how leading does not always need to be out in front and that, yes, it does require courage too. We talked about so many stories she was telling herself, and I was reminded of the stories I needed to tell myself more often, the ones I need to watch for and reframe.

Most of us go through our days telling ourselves stories that go unnoticed and consequently uncorrected. Let's really hear them and determine which are not serving us well. Let's share our inner stories with others, open up and reframe. Are you ready?

1

BELIEVE IT'S POSSIBLE

From "I can't, don't, won't" to **"Just watch me"**

SOPHIE WORKED AT a global consumer goods company and was among a group of high-potential women on a fast track for senior leadership roles within their organization. I was guiding them through their eighteen-month development journey.

From the moment I met Sophie, she struck me as insightful, wise and strategic. Her company knew she was a keeper and was happy to help her relocate several times across Europe to accommodate the demands of her husband's high-level job. She went with the flow of her husband's career and mastered each of her mid-level positions wherever she went. While her aspirations for more simmered under the surface, she hadn't acted on them. Sophie juggled her career and motherhood and, like many, felt torn and that she was not doing either particularly well. Her friends often questioned her decision to work. After all, with her husband's successful career, she didn't "need" to work, did she? Her friends pressured her to be like them: stay-at-home moms married to successful men.

Sophie shared this story with the colleagues at her table during the workshop. The women shook their heads in disbelief and recognition at the same time. Why did her friends' opinions matter when she knew in her heart that she was happy when she worked? In fact, striving for more for herself, having more impact in her company, would only increase her happiness.

As the workshop progressed, Sophie and her colleagues engaged in many conversations that affirmed their strengths and tested their fears. They wrestled with how to tackle barriers in society, in their organizations, in their families and in themselves. The women stoked each other's flames and reminded one another of the marvels they truly were. "You're awesome." "No, *you* are."

Sophie was starting to rethink her own ambitions. During the course of those workshop discussions with supportive, like-minded women, Sophie asked herself a simple question: *Why not me?*

This question also showed up when she asked herself, *Why can't I also aspire to senior leadership positions? Why can't we make it work from a family perspective?* Sophie realized she was tired of waiting for someone to figure it out for her, for permission that it was okay to devote more to her career, for the right time to make a move. She was tired of believing that advancing in her career meant she wasn't a good mother. She decided to believe the time was now and she wasn't going to feel guilty about it anymore.

I saw Sophie's mindset completely change, for good. She stopped questioning her potential and stopped thinking that she shouldn't want and didn't deserve more. She made the decision to aspire for more from her leadership career. She described her perspective shift as the kick in the pants she needed.

From that moment of clarity, Sophie knew it wouldn't be easy to juggle a young family with two working parents in demanding jobs. But that it was *possible* was now crystal clear in her mind.

The results were tangible. Sophie was almost immediately promoted. And then promoted again, and again. After two years, she returned as the executive sponsor of that same high-potential program. She was also included in a magazine feature that named her one of the top thirty business leaders in her country.

So many women don't see the potential and possibility for themselves, like Sophie did. They don't believe they have what it takes, they don't think they deserve it, they don't think it's the right time or they're too exhausted to even consider it.

Have you ever questioned whether it's possible that you are destined for more? That you are capable and deserving of having more impact than you do today?

I sure have. I still do. It's normal.

I waged this battle myself for many years. Early in my career, I worked for a great leader who saw potential in me long before I saw it in myself. He told me I could rise to the senior-most levels of leadership if I wanted. I didn't realize it at the time but having someone voice these words of support was pretty rare; most people go a lifetime without hearing that others believe in them. If you're a people leader, please voice your belief in others, especially women. It could make all the difference for someone. It took me a very long time for those words to fully sink in. Even though he had encouraged and supported me to see my own leadership potential, I doubted that what he said was true. I still ask myself, *What took you so long to believe in yourself, girl?* Imagine what more I could have accomplished if I'd believed sooner, stronger.

Not believing in your potential is a formidable obstacle, but it's never too late to start to challenge this story. Let's explore how to move past the barriers to believing in possibility:

- thinking you don't have what it takes to succeed as a leader
- comparing yourself to others or stale models of leadership
- thinking the risks outweigh the rewards

"I don't belong here"

I was hired to lead a group of aspiring female executives through a leadership development program at a global health sciences company. I asked them to each write down their personal leadership vision: how they wanted leadership to fit into their life, how they wanted to be known as a leader and what specifically they wanted to accomplish. The exercise was meant to build on their strengths, guide their decisions and propel their aspirations. The next step was to say their vision out loud while being video-recorded, sometimes in front of everyone. (I'm so mean, I know, but it really is the best way to learn, and I let people record me all the time, so there.)

"Don't ever make decisions based on fear. Make decisions based on hope and possibility. Make decisions based on what should happen, not what shouldn't."

MICHELLE OBAMA

There was no expectation for the vision to be perfect or even finished; we'd refine and build on the vision over time. The point of the exercise is that when a leader watches her own video, she can see how passionate she is about her vision and if her vision is inspirational, believable and easily shared with others who can help fulfill it.

One by one, the women presented their visions, pausing at the end for self-reflection and supportive feedback from their colleagues. As Megan stood up, we could see she was nervous, more so than most. I smiled at her and said, "Just go for it."

I anticipated debriefing the talk track in her head as she endured the 120 seconds of agony I put her through on camera. But about a minute in, Megan burst into tears. I stopped the camera and asked her what was happening. As I passed Megan a tissue, I asked, "What story are you telling yourself that led to this reaction?" She said that as she looked around at all the amazing women in the room, she couldn't fathom why she was there. She couldn't believe that she was considered to be in the same league as the others. She couldn't believe she was considered a high-potential leader, a future executive. She voiced her biggest fear: that she didn't belong there. Nothing, of course, could have been further from the truth.

Megan had imposter syndrome. Have you ever chalked up your success to luck, chance or good timing? Do you discredit your accomplishments or feel that you don't deserve them? Do you ever feel like a fraud? If you said yes to any of those statements, you may be sabotaging yourself. And before you start putting yourself down for that, guess what: we all do it.

The *Oxford English Dictionary* defines imposter syndrome as the "persistent inability to believe that one's success is deserved or has been legitimately achieved as a result of one's own efforts or skills." Despite evidence of success and competence, there is a persistent fear of being exposed as a fraud. Imposter syndrome erodes your confidence and can prevent you from taking risks or striving for things that you are completely capable of already or are capable of learning.

Research shows that men and women equally experience imposter syndrome. In my experience, though, men don't let imposter syndrome hold them back from trying new things, taking risks and generally going for it. I saw this firsthand, listening to a panel of seasoned experts and executives. The panel consisted of two women and two men; each was given a couple of minutes to introduce themselves. The two women and one man gave a modest introduction of their roles. Dave was last.

In his southern drawl, he said, "Hi, I'm Dave. I don't know what you heard when my fellow panelists just introduced themselves, but here's what I heard. 'I'm Dawn, the brilliant, world-famous doctor at the renowned Mayo Clinic saving people's lives every single day.' 'I'm John, the suave, good-looking and highly educated CEO of a bank.' 'I'm Leslie, the genius scientist working at a multibillion-dollar company you all know and love and I'm saving the world with my discoveries.' And I'm Dave, a hick from Texas who didn't graduate high school, and I help transport stuff."

The audience laughed with shock and disbelief. They didn't expect a man to voice those concerns. After all, Dave belonged up on that stage—right alongside the doctor, CEO and scientist. He had risen to become a company president, he had received awards during his time in the Navy and he's a great leader. He still has doubts about his self-worth in his mind, but he didn't let that stop him. You shouldn't either.

Women's belief that they don't have what it takes to advance into more senior roles is chronic, pervasive and devastating. Global consulting firm Korn Ferry highlighted imposter syndrome in research done in partnership with the Rockefeller Foundation in 2017. In a study to understand how to create a sustainable pipeline of female CEOs, researchers interviewed fifty-seven female CEOs from Fortune 1000 companies or other large privately held companies. These were women who currently or formerly held the CEO position. They had made it to the top—our role models, our beacons of hope.

Wait for it.

The most troubling outcome of the study for me was that despite having tremendous potential, the majority of women CEOs who participated in the study had never seen the role of CEO as a possibility for themselves. In fact, a shocking 65 percent of the women in the study said they never thought they could be CEO until someone told them they had what it took. A mere 9 percent said they had always wanted the top position.

I know that not everyone wants to be CEO or a senior leader. That's fine. But that women at every level don't believe that the CEO position is *possible* for them is heartbreaking.

The 2015 KPMG Women's Leadership Study, conducted by the independent research company Ipsos, sought to understand how the aspiration and ambition to lead was developed and nurtured—or not— in women. Ipsos surveyed 3,014 US women (2,410 professional working women and 604 women in college) between the ages of eighteen and sixty-four. Among the findings were these disheartening statistics: 67 percent of women said they need more support building confidence to feel like they can be leaders; 59 percent said they sometimes find it hard to see themselves as a leader.

The lack of confidence these women felt also affects an array of other activities tied to becoming a leader or seeking new and interesting projects. The women said they do not feel confident to ask for sponsors (92 percent), to seek mentors (79 percent), to ask for access to senior leadership (76 percent), to pursue a job opportunity beyond their experience (73 percent), to ask for a career path plan (69 percent) or to request a promotion (65 percent), a raise (61 percent) or a new role or position (56 percent).

If you identify with any of these findings, then not only are you in the majority, but you also need to keep reading this book! Women need to start seeing themselves as leadership material and going after the opportunities and experiences that will grow their skills and confidence, so they can take their rightful places in leadership roles. I get it: we often don't have role models and we are often shut out. But we can't believe we don't belong there.

I've had the fortune of meeting many women who have persevered and broken through to leadership roles in part because they believed they could. It shouldn't have been as hard a battle as it was, and the number of women in these positions is too small. These women tell me they feel alone because there are too few women surrounding them at this leadership level. They desperately wish more women would join them, despite the obstacles they will encounter. Until we *feel* like we belong in senior positions, we can't begin to collectively fight the barriers, stereotypes and biases that hold us back.

"I'm not as good as they are"

Recall Megan, who burst into tears during her leadership vision recording. Not only did she doubt her potential, but she also compared herself to the other high-potential women in the program and deemed herself not worthy. Everyone in the room had unique strengths. For some reason, Megan didn't think hers were as valuable. When Megan's colleagues heard her voice the concern that she wasn't as deserving as them, they were gobsmacked. They considered her a scientific genius. One woman responded by saying, "Megan, I'm in sales; I sell things. I manage people who sell things. You, like, invent things!" Megan was the reason the rest of them had things to sell, market and manage. She'd let her own insecurities and comparisons lead to toxic thoughts about her potential as a leader.

Megan is not alone. Chronic comparing is something women do. Have you ever been disheartened by someone's presentation prowess or career progress, lusted over someone's home or handbag or rolled your eyes at the results of someone's perfect fitness program? It's likely. From *Good Housekeeping* in the 1950s to the beauty and fashion industry to Pinterest and Instagram, comparison is a well-engrained practice of most women.

There are real consequences to such comparison. It creates unrealistic expectations of how we should look, act and spend our time, and it undermines our confidence. The reality is that no one's life or journey is perfect or easy. Everyone has their own challenges, obstacles and demons. Guess what: that perfectly poised executive went through moments of feeling downright terrified. That presentation that flowed so effortlessly went through many rounds of editing and constructive feedback. And the most inspiring people are always those regular folks who succeeded despite their hardships, not the ones who had a leg up to begin with or who seemingly glided through life. Decide to believe you are every bit as good as them. Damn it, you're probably better. And if we learned anything from the story of Megan, the brilliant scientist, they're probably looking at you and silently admiring your awesomeness too.

"I don't want to take the risk"

Deciding to believe in possibility and in your potential requires that you take risks. It can be scary to go for it. Many women mull over opportunities to learn or advance and decide it's just not worth it. The cons outweigh the pros. The fear of the unknown paralyzes us. When we don't exactly understand the opportunity or know if we'll be good at it, we decide to believe it's not possible.

The 2019 KPMG Women's Leadership Study that surveyed more than two thousand US women showed that taking career risks was an area where women fell short. Just over half of the women (55 percent) believe those who do take more career risks progress more quickly. I would have thought that number to be higher. While the women in the survey cited the benefits of increased risk-taking— such as career advancement, personal development and building respect among colleagues—only 43 percent were open to taking bigger risks associated with career advancement, such as asking for a promotion or a raise or moving for a job. Women were more comfortable taking risks that benefit the organization or group, and less so when only benefiting themselves.

When asked what has contributed most to their personal and professional success, women identified qualities such as working hard, being detail oriented and organized. They were less likely to cite more personal character attributes, like being strong-willed or a good leader. I'm thinking a little self-praise is in order right about now. Good thing that's coming in chapter 5.

Risk-taking was toward the bottom of the list of contributions to success for women in the study. When asked what concerned the women about taking risks or prevented them from taking action, the top responses were: looking like I don't know as much as I should, being ignored or not taken seriously, failing at something I try and looking like I'm doing something or saying something that isn't smart. And sadly, while women's confidence and wisdom grow as they progress in their career, risk-taking declines as women age.

Do you sympathize with these women? Do you see yourself in some of these findings? What is preventing you from deciding to believe in what's possible? Let's see if we can find out.

Activity: Your possibility story

Let's pause and think about what you truly believe is possible for you. What stories are you telling yourself that help you and that hinder you? This activity asks you to reflect on the constraints and barriers you put forward that may be blocking your chances to experience further success in your career, however you define success for yourself. Take a few moments to answer the following questions.

What do you believe is possible for you?

_____

_____

_____

What makes you feel this way? Think of evidence of past successes and barriers or constraints, both past and future.

_____

_____

_____

What would you like to change about your possibility story?

_____

_____

_____

Reframes

Let's look at how to shift unhelpful mindsets, so you can tell yourself a different story about what is possible for you. Let's move from closed, constrained and fixed to wide-open, redefining and fluid.

From doubt and disbelief to "bank on me"

Do you believe it's possible for you to accomplish more, master a new skill or change career tracks completely? If you don't believe it's possible, then it's important to know where your belief originates.

Megan told herself a story that she wasn't senior leadership material, especially in comparison to other women whom she perceived to be smarter or more deserving. Megan suffered from what the psychologist Albert Bandura called low self-efficacy.

Self-efficacy is a personal belief about our ability to complete a particular task. Leadership self-efficacy refers to an individual's belief in their ability to succeed as a leader. Megan's organization had already identified her as a successful mid-level leader, but she could not fathom she had what it took to advance further. That was Megan's starting point. Her development journey had to begin with gaining confidence in her strengths before she could move forward with anything else. She needed to believe in herself by understanding what skills and challenges lay ahead and that she had the tool kit to learn and tackle them as she had in the past. The good news is that low self-efficacy can be overcome.

A team from the Center for Women's Health Research from the University of Wisconsin–Madison engaged in a study examining whether leadership self-efficacy could be increased for women in STEMM (science, technology, engineering, mathematics and medicine). The team knew that many interventions are needed to counteract the pervasive stereotypes that limit women's entry, persistence and advancement in academic STEMM. However, they wanted to explore what impact an individual educational intervention would have. They wanted to see if they could change the beliefs of women in these fields and spur them to action. Behavior change was what they were after. Would these women, still early in their careers, remain, persevere and essentially go for it in a field that was stacked against them?

The team created a sixteen-week course that included learning about gender biases in themselves and others and how to neutralize them. They participated in presentations, discussions and mentor meetings to build self-efficacy, as well as learned through weekly journaling and case studies and by applying course material to real-world situations.

Quantitative and qualitative results of this study did indeed show increases in the women's leadership self-efficacy, personal mastery and self-esteem. It also showed a decrease in perceived constraints. The program helped the women tell themselves a different story. They believed in what was possible and they were spurred to action. The study results also suggest that the women felt more empowered to identify and reduce the influence of gender bias in their professional lives.

I saw this same transformation while working with a group of female senior managers at a global professional services firm. The program was a year-long development initiative that included many of the same elements as the study above. During a workshop, we did the same leadership vision video-recorded activity I described to you earlier in the chapter with Megan. This time it was Svetlana, a smart, driven young leader who had an equally profound, but quite different, reaction during the activity.

As she began, it sounded like Svetlana was reading a prepared speech. This often happens with type A personalities. They write the perfect prose and, damn it, they don't want to miss a single word of their masterpiece. Svetlana fell into this trap and focused more on her content than on her delivery. I jotted down feedback about believability and delivering a message with passion and heart, which I would provide when she finished.

But then something happened. About halfway through the recording, Svetlana's whole demeanor changed. It was palpable. While she didn't miss a beat in her content, her eyes suddenly lit up. She spoke faster, and she smiled. I could have sworn she even stood taller. All of a sudden she was delivering her vision with passion and from the heart. Go, girl!

When she finished, I could hardly wait to ask Svetlana what happened to cause the change in her delivery. What was she telling herself that differed so dramatically from the minute prior?

Svetlana said that as she listened to herself speak her vision aloud, she started to believe it. She felt the shift herself and said, "I believe that I can become the leader I am describing." What was at first merely aspirational became possible. Her eyes became sparkly with tears. We all choked up in happiness for her. Her mindset shifted. She saw the possibility and it showed.

Svetlana's transformation was a bit different from Megan's. Svetlana was confident in her current abilities and wanted to advance into more senior positions. She was excited to be selected for the high-potential program; she believed she belonged there and couldn't wait to progress. But she couldn't quite envision what that looked like or how she would step into it. Svetlana's development journey was about stretching herself into more complex situations to gain confidence in herself as a senior leader. She still had to build self-efficacy, but her focus was on fulfilling her own vision.

Sophie's story was different again. Recall from this chapter's opening story that she had a sense of confidence in her abilities. She likely even knew that opportunities were abundant for her should she want them. Sophie's belief in the possible was limited by how she would make it happen from a whole life and family perspective. She had a young family and a husband who was in a demanding job. It wasn't about if she could advance; it was about how it would play out if she did. When she asked herself, *Why not me?*, she was tired of putting her ambitions on the back burner.

Sophie ultimately made the decision to ask for more from her career. She wanted to have more impact now, not when her kids were older. She knew this would mean increased pressure from having more responsibility, feeling uncomfortable in the unknown and spending time away from family. She knew she and her husband would be doing a lot more juggling. They got good at it fast because they had to. They didn't want to repeat the nightmare that happened the morning they realized they were both getting ready to go to the airport to board separate business flights. A new caregiver was starting that morning, and no one would be home to greet her. After that, they became a well-oiled machine.

Whatever your starting point, figure out what your beliefs are about what is possible for you. Revisit your answers to the questions in the possibility story activity and consider:

- What fears and constraints did you note?
- Which of those are internal and which are external?
- What is in your control to change?
- How can you decide to believe in your potential and what's truly possible?

Belief in your own potential—that you can succeed in roles with more responsibility, greater risk or higher profile—is the first step. Decide to believe it's possible. It starts there.

Once you get to that place of possibility, please, please help the women and girls around you to see their own potential and what is possible for them. Help others tell themselves a different story.

From caught in comparison to "carve the path"
. . . .

When it comes to leadership specifically, maybe we are comparing ourselves to the wrong ideal. Actually, I'm pretty sure we are. There is a global phenomenon called "think manager, think male." It is a well-researched stereotype that results in us automatically associating men and masculine characteristics with leadership. We all do this. Sadly, not only does this tendency result in biases that prevent women from ascending into more leadership roles, but it also undervalues the many qualities that are required for leadership today.

Author Tomas Chamorro-Premuzic, the chief talent scientist at ManpowerGroup, argues that many men end up in leadership positions that they really shouldn't be in. In his book *Why Do So Many Incompetent Men Become Leaders? (And How to Fix It)*, he writes, "We need to have leaders who are competent, humble and ethical. Since men tend to be on average more confident . . . and more narcissistic, this also explains why so many men, especially of the incompetent variety, end up in leadership roles when they shouldn't."

Research shows that women tend to score higher on most leadership capabilities, despite the "think manager, think male" stereotype. I hear many organizations say they value teamwork, collaboration, talent development and emotional intelligence. Yet the senior leadership ranks are still a pit of toxic posturing, bullying and egotism. There is mounting research that shows that women-led companies, or companies with a 50/50 executive gender split, have more engaged employees. Women-owned companies are also shown to have higher returns, and new research shows that when women are brought into the C-suite, they shift how the organization thinks about innovation, which in turn results in more value-creating strategies.

It's clear the world needs more women in leadership. We need to redefine what good leadership looks like. Don't compare yourself to the old model; the old model in many respects is broken or unbearable.

Colleen fell into the trap of comparing herself to an old and uncomfortable model of leadership. She told her story to a group of women in a workshop I ran. We were discussing the topic of feedback when someone asked what to do when they get feedback they don't agree with.

Colleen responded with "sometimes you know better and you need the courage to do your own thing." Colleen shared a story of receiving feedback from her boss who said she was too soft and didn't drive results hard enough. Her boss was a self-proclaimed bulldozer when the situation called for it. He talked a good game about having straight-up conversations that called people on behaviors or decisions, but she suspected that he either didn't have these conversations at all, or when he did, he just talked and didn't listen. He avoided conversations until he boiled over and then exploded. Conversations with him were one-sided. She knew this because she was on the receiving end at times. He would ask for feedback but when he received it, he either defended or discounted it. Colleen saw the impacts of this as her boss became known as difficult and uncollaborative in the organization. It didn't seem to bother him; he said he was getting things done. Colleen knew that he wasn't as effective or influential as he thought he was or as he could have been.

And now it seemed to Colleen that he was asking her to be more like him. It felt inauthentic and plain wrong. Colleen knew that there were other ways to be effective. She too had tough conversations with others when required, but she listened a lot more than she talked. She continued to build relationships with colleagues, so that when she did have to "get tough," it felt easier. People believed her when she said she acted in their best interests; the team or the organization was always at the center of these conversations.

Colleen took much of her boss's feedback to heart and made many changes that helped her become a better leader. But she decided to downright disregard this piece of feedback and model a different kind of leadership.

From ducking the risks to "seize the rewards"

Many women overlook the fact that there is much to gain from stretching yourself and taking risks to grow and to advance.

First, continuous learning. Growth as we're challenged in new ways is at the heart of being human. Achieving staves off boredom and reminds us of what it is to be alive. It makes us braver to press on to new challenges, creating a positive cycle that reduces fear.

Marissa, a successful consultant, knew this to be the case when she applied for and started a doctoral program in the middle of a pandemic... with six kids... three of whom were under the age of twelve. People thought she was crazy, me included, at first. But as Marissa explained it, it made complete sense. Her personal vision always included earning a doctorate. She wants to teach and write and coach. She's doing some of that now but not in the way she wants to be, the way she's fully capable of. I asked her how she felt about the impending juggle with three kids at home doing virtual schooling, her own rigorous courses and her work keeping clients happy. Marissa thought long and hard about the decision to start her PhD now. She knew in her heart that fulfilling her dreams and her personal vision would bring her the most happiness. The heart-ache of waiting until the three younger kids were more independent would be worse than the increased chaos of her house. Marissa is energized when she reads research and discusses it in her learning pods. It's not a chore; it's her joy. It doesn't drain her; it buoys her. At times, she confesses, it's the best part of her day.

I'm not suggesting that you should, right now, chose to under-take the hardest possible task for yourself like Marissa did. What I'm suggesting is that you open up to stretching yourself. Don't con-cede to the automatic thought that stretching, growing, advancing inevitably bring more madness. In fact, it might be the beacon that pulls you through.

The second reward advancement can bring is impact. It feels good to have bigger and broader impact on customers, patients, organizations, cultures and communities. This is the essence of leadership. If you desire to have a broader impact, there's no better way than to get in front of wide-reaching issues and vexing problems. It is rewarding to shape the experiences of employees and customers and to make decisions that influence your organization, your sector or policies that create better outcomes.

Third, increased earning potential. Although dual-income families are the norm today, the majority of women depend on joint earnings or a partner's earnings for a sense of financial stability. But life has a way of sneaking up on us. Loved ones get sick, leave or pass on. Kids stay in school longer or depend on their parents longer. Sallie Krawcheck, one of the highest-ranked women ever to work on Wall Street and author of *Own It*, reminds us why women need real financial independence. We retire with two-thirds the money that men have and live five-plus years longer. Career breaks are expensive beyond the lost salary in the leave years. They compound exponentially. A woman, for example, who earns $80,000 a year and takes a two-year break will lose more than $1 million over the course of her career. Money shouldn't be the only driver, of course, and that's why the other benefits are important too. If we only work for money in a stressful position, burnout is inevitable, and no one wants that.

Last, but certainly not least, the world needs more women as leadership role models to show the way for other women and girls. I was genuinely surprised to receive comments about being a role model when I held a senior leadership position. I was taken aback when people reached out to me and said how refreshing it was to see a senior leader like me. I was a woman; I was authentic and approachable; I had a family. In their eyes, that was not the norm. Here's what I told these young women when they asked how I managed the juggle: with some difficulty and many lessons along the way. There's no magic formula, but many things we can learn from one another. Once I decided it was possible, it became so. It's possible for you too. It's truly possible.

1:1:1 Plan

Once a week

- **Yell yet.** When you think of something that you haven't done, haven't accomplished or think you can't do, add the word *yet*. Instead of saying, "I don't know anything about that," say, "I don't know anything about that *yet*." Don't discount the possibly of gaining new knowledge, experience or expertise. Say it loud and proud.

- **Tune in.** Catch yourself when you start to say, "I can't, won't, don't, shouldn't," etc. Reflect on what leads you to automatically default to this way of thinking. Reframe and think about what is needed for you to say "I can, I will, I may, I am" instead.

- **Affirm, don't deny.** Capture self-affirming statements by saying them aloud and writing them down. These can be related to your strengths, your goals, your wins—however big or small. These statements feed positive stories in our mind.

Once a month

- **Be in the clouds.** Aspire. Make a wish; pursue an aim. Let your mind wander. Cast hope for something intellectual, professional, spiritual, physical. It doesn't matter. Give yourself permission to dream: it makes the impossible possible. Be bold. Take a deep breath. Isn't that awesome?

- **Rewire your fail circuit.** Look back on a "failure" or when something didn't go as you hoped. How are you thinking about that experience? Do you blame yourself? Do you attribute the event to your personal failure, to a flaw in your intelligence or character? If so, reframe the event to understand that it resulted due to insufficient experience or knowledge and that you have the power to learn and apply different principles, actions or skills the next time. Learn from it and move on; don't dwell on it and stay stuck.

- **Compare back.** Think of a time when you compared yourself to someone else and you came out on the negative end. First, remind yourself that this behavior is leading to an unhealthy mindset. Next, recall your strengths and your positive attributes. Remind yourself of all you have learned. Compare back to a younger you, not to others. Then remind yourself that nobody is perfect. Reset your comparison to yourself and how you will continue to learn, advance and grow in your own way at your own time. Master self-compassion.

Once a year

- **Prove possible.** Look back to notice what you have accomplished that seemed impossible only weeks, months or years before. Relish in the fact that you tried something, accomplished something. Regardless of how it turned out, you made the impossible feel possible.

- **Seek a spark.** If you need a little boost of inspiration, go online and watch something that lifts you up. Examples include the Nike "Dream Crazier" commercial, Notre Dame coach Muffet McGraw explaining why we need more women in power or a TED Talk by someone you find motivating. Internalize the messages and think about how you can use the inspiration to further your goals, aspirations and feeling of possibility.

- **Ponder your possibility story.** Redo the possibility story activity on page 30 and gauge how you feel about having the highest levels of success in your career. What mindsets are helping you and which are hindering you? What supports can you bolster and what constraints need to be addressed?

Which reframe was most useful for you in this chapter on possibility?

From _____ to _____ .

2
LOOK UP, LOOK OUT

From "I'll worry about it later" to **"I shape my future today"**

THE WORKSHOP PARTICIPANTS at a large financial institution were enjoying the requisite continental breakfast before the session began. It was the appointed networking hour when the women got to meet other leaders who had advanced in their organization. They chatted in small groups and took turns introducing themselves to the senior leaders. June, a seasoned executive and role model for many women in the organization, was making the rounds before she kicked off the workshop. At the top of her game in a male-dominated field, she was a beacon of hope for many female colleagues aspiring to advance. Meeting her in person, the women were inspired by her authenticity and approachable demeanor. She was real and very much like them. We were all excited to hear her words of wisdom.

June didn't disappoint during her prepared speech. She outlined her leadership journey, her challenges and how she overcame them. She motivated the group to believe in themselves and feel that anything was possible. Everyone was feeling pumped.

Then came the Q&A. June responded to the typical questions about work-life balance and operating in male-dominated meetings. Her answers were honest, at times witty. A mid-level leader asked June how she had charted her path to the top. The aspiring leader knew it was important to be deliberate about her career goals and was looking for sage guidance on how to move into more senior roles.

June thought for a moment and then said that she really hadn't had a plan and just kind of fell into one role after another. She had some sponsorship along the way that was critical to her advancement, leaders who had guided her and tapped her on the shoulder. But she laughed nervously and finished with, "Sometimes I look back and wonder, *How* did *I get here?*"

I cringed and withered inside. *Noooo, this is what happens when clients don't let me prep the speakers,* I thought. All the air was sucked out of the room. In an industry with too few female role models at the top, the one they revered seemed to be there by luck. The women looked up to June, yet they walked away feeling that she chalked up her success to chance and her good fortune to have men pull her up the organization. Of course, we know how critical a role a sponsor—a senior person with decision-making power and influence who advocates for someone in a more junior position—plays for anyone looking to advance. But June's response negated any feeling that women had control in shaping their career destinies. June couldn't comment on the tough conversations of self-advocacy with which the women were struggling. She couldn't provide insight on struggling, failing and trying again. She couldn't guide them on the creation of a career plan as they strive to realize a larger vision of self-fulfillment.

June did provide lots of valuable tips and strategies on how to succeed at the executive table. But unfortunately, her inspirational kickoff to the workshop fell flat because none of the aspiring leaders gained insight into how to get there with purpose and deliberateness. If it was all up to chance, then what were they even doing in the workshop? I know this because it was a hot topic of reflection during the workshop discussions that followed.

June was being genuine. She was an authentic leader and her conversation with the female leaders in the workshop was great ... until it wasn't. Sadly, June's account of her journey is consistent with that of many women who have risen to the top.

A recent study done by the Working Mother Research Institute and its National Association for Female Executives (NAFE) division looked at the experiences of women at all levels of corporations to determine what perceptions and realities keep them out of the highest ranks. They found that women were less likely than men to know how they wanted their careers to advance. Women did not have a vision for their future and were less likely to understand or have access to information on career paths. Women were less aware of development programs or opportunities, such as mentorship and sponsorship, and less likely to engage in those opportunities. If they had a mentor, women were also less likely to engage in a career discussion with them.

What is crystal clear is that no one should leave their development and career up to chance or in the hands of others. The bigger concern I have is the pattern of women not reflecting enough on what it is they want or not looking further out. Without a clear horizon in your eyeline, you are left stumbling through the day, head down, attempting to avoid mistakes, missteps and exhaustion.

Enter the personal vision. A personal vision helps by presenting a compelling image of an achievable future. It describes the kind of leader you want to be and the kind of impact and influence you want to have. It focuses your attention on what matters most to you personally and professionally. It calls you toward a larger purpose and what you want to accomplish. It is easily articulated as a statement or a short paragraph, or even a graphic vision board. It can contain a particular role or title, but it doesn't have to. You keep this vision on the horizon as a beacon to move toward, at whatever pace works for you.

Can you articulate your personal vision? Do you have goals for your development and your future? Are you working toward a longer-term future on the horizon? Do you spend more time planning a vacation than you do your career? I bet you have a bucket list of travel destinations but not a bucket list of career positions.

As one partner of a top global consulting firm said to me, "I know what all the men on my team want. They're constantly telling me, updating me on their wins and asking for opportunities. Sometimes, yes, it's too much information and prodding from the men, but at least I know. I have *no* clue what the women on my team want. I'm not sure they know either."

Why is this the case for many women? In my experience, the lack of a personal vision boils down to three elements:

- balancing professional ambition and caretaking roles
- maintaining unreasonable expectations of themselves
- emphasizing learning at the cost of clearer goals

"I just gotta get through today"

Do you count the hours until you can crack open a bottle of wine or reach for the remote to binge on Netflix? Do you await the weekend and holidays like a four-year-old does Christmas morning? When you lie in bed willing yourself to sleep, do you thank the gods that you made it through the day? If you do, I get it. We all feel that way at times. One reason is that women spread their time and energy across more domains than men. We perform triple, quadruple, or quintuple duty with work, home, school, elder care, volunteering and so on and so on.

We know from numerous research studies that women still carry the burden of caretaking responsibilities with the home and family. Socially, women are also not only expected to be the ones to engage in these duties, but they are also judged more harshly for how well they are performed. Doing double duty at work and at home keeps women in the torrent of getting through the day, leaving little time to focus on career or longer-term goals to build toward future happiness.

Olivia knew this all too well despite her continuous drive for achievement, as she pursued advanced degrees and admired role models. After her dad died when she was a teenager, she watched as her stay-at-home mom reeducated herself and reentered the workforce. A career and an education were important to Olivia. She relished achieving and wanted to continue to achieve, which fed her confidence.

Like most young professionals, she entered the workforce after her post-graduate studies; she was trying to figure out what achieving meant and what she wanted to do. Olivia worked at top companies in her industry and consulting before "life took over." Her husband became the primary breadwinner; given his career in investment banking, Olivia said it was unlikely she could make as much money as he was making and would continue to make. She had a child and then another, and life got in the way of her figuring out how to achieve.

Olivia went back to work part-time in a good job, but it was not intellectually challenging. She regularly felt the guilt and the pull between her two focuses. Olivia wanted to have a meaningful foot in the door at home and still work on interesting projects that built toward a future when the kids were grown. Her husband would call her the VP of home operations in a show of support, illustrating how much he appreciated her efforts as he spent more and more time at work, building his career at the critical promotion points. But it pissed her off to no end and she told him to just cut it out! This was compounded by others who showed their "support" by commenting that she was capable of so much more. That made her angry too. She felt internal and external pressure about what she should be doing. She wondered if she was trying to meet everyone else's expectations at the expense of her own.

Olivia's story is many women's story, illustrating the pull that women with children have between their families and their career aspirations. But it's not only women with children who rarely look to the future: many women without children have not created a bold longer-term vision for themselves either. We all have work to do here. I have observed, in general, that women are more reticent to articulate aspirations—whether it's a dream job or experiences they'd like to gain. The challenge is that when others (especially men) put their requests out there ("I want that role"; "I want to be on that project"; "I want to take part in that meeting"), it is more likely it will happen and that they'll have sponsorship along the way.

For a long time, many believed, and sadly still do, that women inherently suffer an ambition gap, especially when they have children. Thankfully, recent studies are disproving this. Boston

Consulting Group (BCG) surveyed 200,000 employees, including 141,000 women from 189 countries, and found women to be as ambitious as men at the beginning of their careers. It was the company they worked for that impacted their ambition, not family status or motherhood. At firms where employees felt the company was the least progressive on gender diversity, the ambition gap between women and men aged thirty to forty was 17 percent. At these firms, only 66 percent of women sought promotions compared with 83 percent of men. But at firms where employees felt gender diversity was improving, there was almost no ambition gap between women and men aged thirty to forty. At these firms, 85 percent of women sought promotions compared with 87 percent of men.

What this BCG study reinforced was that while having children or being responsible for caretaking may make it more difficult to juggle priorities, it's not the primary reason women are not advancing, and it certainly doesn't mean they lack ambition.

I have heard several female executives express regret that they didn't plan more. In fact, many studies exploring the hurdles to advancement for women documented women wishing they had discovered and undertaken career planning earlier. When you reflect on your values, desires, strengths and gaps, you can then be more mindful about choosing the right development and support tools to achieve long-term personal and professional growth, including those organizations that will support you. Planning makes the hurdles feel less high. Working toward something bigger makes each day feel less like a slog. It makes you more purposeful and boosts your self-confidence as you take steps toward it. Rising to the top (if that's your goal) feels more possible.

And yet too few women think about their longer-term vision and what they're striving for personally and professionally. We plan our careers in short increments and trudge through day by day, week by week until the years roll by and we say, "How did I end up here?" Are you stuck in getting through the day instead of lifting your head and looking out to tomorrow? Do you say to yourself, *I'll think about that later*?

"I'm not ready"

Another reason women stay stuck is that they tend to expect more from themselves and set the criteria for promotion too high. This translates into a mistaken belief that they don't have what it takes to succeed in a role with elements they haven't yet demonstrated proficiency in. Having high expectations, on its face, seems like an excellent way to operate. But I was curious whether this tendency may in fact be holding some women back from seizing opportunities, living up to their potential or from fulfilling their personal vision. It seems it might.

In a study published in the *American Sociological Review*, Shelley Correll examined the constraining effect of cultural beliefs about gender on the emerging career aspirations of men and women. The study asked eighty first-year undergraduate students to complete two rounds of tasks measuring a fictitious ability. The students believed the test was career relevant; they were told the task was developed by a national testing organization and of interest to graduate schools and Fortune 500 companies. But the test had no right answers and in fact was impossible to complete correctly.

Correll hypothesized that women were likely to judge themselves by tougher standards than men, lowering their self-assessments and their related career aspirations. Ugh, unfortunately, her hypothesis was proven true in this study.

What Correll found was that when participants were told that women were less competent than men at a task (which—remember— was actually fake and impossible to complete), women judged their performance more negatively, set higher standards for what proficiency in the task looked like and expressed much less interest in a course, seminar, graduate program or high-paying job that would require the same skills as the task. When participants were told they performed the same, women and men judged their performance near equal and created similar standards for high performance. When deemed equal at the task, women expressed more interest in career aspirations related to the task than men.

When exposed to negative gender stereotypes, women judge themselves harsher. Leaders and organizations need to support cultures that take gender out of the equation. And women need to stop the toxic comparison that this study highlights.

This study shines a light on something I have seen over and over. Women believe they need to be absolutely fantastic at something—even an expert—before wading further into the unknown. They set unrealistically high expectations for themselves; when they don't meet them, they give up or stay stuck in their comfort zone. Have you done this? One common area this shows up is in job applications. Women tend to wait until they meet most of the qualifications for a job before applying (if they even apply), while men tend to apply if they meet only some (or even none) of the qualifications.

Ask yourself, Am I missing out because I'm afraid I'm not good enough? Am I prematurely saying no to opportunities because I believe I'm inherently not right for them? Am I selling myself short? Am I not creating a longer-term plan because I can't envision all that I can accomplish? In the words of Olivia (to her husband who gave her a home VP title), "Just cut it out!" Meanwhile, as Correll's study showed, so many people are out there doing it with the same or much less expertise, experience and knowledge than you. It's time to go for it.

"I just want to keep learning"

The workshops I run include a segment on articulating your personal vision—the dreaded video-recording activity. When I begin these vision exercises, the default reaction from most women is "I don't know!" I often hear "I just want to keep learning." Don't get me wrong, learning is a great thing. But there has to be a target for the learning in a professional setting. Otherwise you might as well pick up a set of encyclopedias at a yard sale and soak up the knowledge. Enter trivia contests; maybe try out for *Jeopardy!*

The Hay Group highlighted learning for learning's sake in its study focusing on the performance and career paths of twelve of

"I've learned that making a 'living' is not the same as making a 'life.'"

MAYA ANGELOU

the highest-positioned women leaders in one Fortune 500 company and other female executives in global organizations. The study found that both high-performing men and women had a strong orientation toward achievement. However, for women it manifested more as a lifelong focus on continuous learning. A commitment to lifelong learning is a wonderful trait and did help the women prepare for future roles at higher levels, but it's even more helpful when directed intentionally toward a concrete purpose.

The Hay Group study found that for women the learning trait did not necessarily lead to proactive career management: women were less deliberate in their career progressions than men and still had a way to go in driving specific efforts toward a goal. The study described the thought patterns of women as a generic desire to learn, grow and build capabilities. What's needed instead, it argued, is a purposeful thought pattern: intentionally create opportunities to learn a specific skill and gain exact experience to earn a particular position.

The other way I've seen this play out is when women seek to educate or skill themselves so thoroughly in an effort to shore up confidence before they ascend into positions with more responsibility. In the United States, women hold nearly 60 percent of advanced degrees yet still hold fewer executive positions and bring home less pay. I have had countless conversations with women who want to get another master's degree or a PhD, or take yet another course or certification. I begin by asking them what purpose it will serve. Are the credentials required to achieve your vision or are they required only to live up to your own expectations? Are the money, time and effort involved really worth it when you haven't yet showcased the amazing talent and skills you already possess? I'm not knocking advanced education, skill development or certification in the slightest. They are valuable. My worry is when women use them as a crutch that they don't need in the first place, or when they feel like knowledge outweighs experience. Do you put off going for it when you may already have exactly what you need inside that big brain of yours?

The Hay Group study also found that the mindset of continuous general learning can drive career advancement to a point, but it often leaves women relying on others to steer opportunities toward specific positions. Women, in essence, weren't driving their own success, nor steering their own career advancement. Much like June from the beginning of this chapter, the women in this study described their careers as "happening to them," which may produce the results you want, but it also may not. We work for decades, a long time. You deserve to shape your career, your time, your energy. You deserve to be where you want to be.

Activity: Your horizon story

Imagining many years into the future is a challenging task to be sure. But you must begin somewhere, and remember that you can change your answers anytime. Let's start by seeing what stories you're telling yourself today about tomorrow. Ponder your future self. Maybe you're at your retirement party, or you're reminiscing as an elder on a beach or you're witnessing your own funeral (yes, that is a real thought experiment people do). Embrace your gray hair and wrinkles and all the wisdom that it brings. Now answer the questions below.

What legacy have you created for yourself? (Think of your impact and what you are known for.)

_____

_____

_____

What competencies (skills, knowledge and abilities) did you learn and leverage?

_____

_____

_____

What advice would you give your younger self (that's you, today)?

_____

_____

_____

How can you put yourself into a better place to learn and stretch today?

_____

_____

_____

What can you do now to take even the smallest step toward that legacy?

_____

_____

_____

Reframes

Merely getting through the day is not a satisfying way to live. You have the opportunity to change the feeling of drudgery, grind or drifting. Let's explore how to live purposely by looking up and further out on the horizon. Let's look at how to take small steps to a fulfilling future, embrace stretching and learning and remain flexible while making conscious decisions. While the grind may not disappear, it will feel less meaningless. And that is a good thing.

From stuck in survive to "free to thrive"

If you feel like you're trudging through the days, you might also describe yourself as stuck in a rut: same old work days, same old dinner, same old drop-offs, same old haircut. It's hard to work toward something new or different when you're stuck in the same old, same old. It's also harder to feel engaged in your work when you're trapped in the same patterns.

A larger vision of your future can increase your engagement and get you unstuck. As Olivia, the VP of home operations (sigh), is coming out of the toddler zone, she's working this out for herself. She's building toward a longer-term vision but needs smaller, present-day steps to keep the feelings of guilt and overwhelm in check. She's starting to take on more projects at work, including launching a new product and coauthoring a book. Because she is a high achiever, she's offered a lot of opportunities. She told me that the hardest part is finding balance. She doesn't want to keep getting completely sucked in at work or at home. She makes small movements, which helps her feel less guilt. It takes a lot of discipline to say no to things, or "thank you, not yet." But Olivia has faith that opportunities will continue to arise because she adds tremendous value and she's keeping an eye on shaping her future.

I valued my conversations with Olivia, the *former* VP of home operations, so much that I took her a care package. It contained instructions to send the dog, the two kids and her husband outside for a long, long walk while she indulged in brownies, bubbly and *Tiger King*. She deserved it. The way Olivia continues to look up and out inspired me too.

Olivia is like many women who became less deliberate in their career decision-making when family planning years took over. But if you're worried about the repercussion of taking leaves in the short term, take solace in the words of some seasoned female CEOs.

A team of researchers reported on an in-depth study of twelve female CEOs of global corporations. One recommendation these women wanted to share was to focus on the long-term goal. The female CEOs were well aware of the trade-offs of work and family but insisted that missing out on a few years in your career is not the end of the world as long as you plan for it. Take the time you need but don't walk away, they urged. Come back and resume pursuit of your goals. Sure, others may have jumped ahead a bit in the meantime, but there's time to catch up. A career is a long haul. Don't wander through it unconsciously.

Having a personal vision not only helps you get unstuck, but also enhances meaningful and lasting engagement in your chosen path.

Researchers Kathleen Buse and Diana Bilimoria examined how personal vision enhanced the engagement and retention of women in the engineering profession, which suffers from a notorious lack of women. The shortage stems from women not pursuing the profession in school, not pursing the career even if they have an engineering degree or dropping out once they are working in the profession.

The authors were curious to understand what made women stay in engineering. They found that women who persisted in engineering had a personal vision that included their profession, and that the vision enabled them to overcome the biases, barriers and discrimination in the engineering workplace. They validated that a personal vision means having a picture of one's ideal self and comprises a core identity, hope, optimism and self-efficacy.

The authors proposed that energy, efforts and, at times, sacrifices are made in the short term to accomplish more important longer-term goals to achieve the personal vision, or the future ideal self. Also, women who persisted were engaged in their work when they were doing meaningful, worthwhile, useful or valuable work. The women described being continuously challenged and having positive interactions with others.

Interestingly, the authors found that the reasons women stayed were not the inverse of why women left the profession. While women who left cited difficult work conditions and environments, such as unsupportive organizational practices, the women who stayed faced those same challenges. They remained because they were engaged and found meaning. They kept their eye on the horizon by working toward their personal vision, their ideal self.

Their research busted another important myth. Many have suggested that women will trade a challenging job for work-home balance and thus leave the profession when more balance is desired. However, this study suggests that women will find the appropriate balance when they are appropriately challenged and find meaning and engagement in their work. Often it is cited that women leave the workforce to have a family or support their partner's career. However, most women in the study's sample were married (63 percent); for women over thirty, 79 percent were married. More than three-quarters of the women over thirty had at least one child, and 63 percent had two or more children. Further, the number of children had no direct impact on either engagement or career commitment, with the exception that women with more children increased their commitment to engineering as they aged.

Melanie makes the point of keeping her eye on the horizon abundantly clear. She is a senior manager at a large telecommunications company. She is smart, assertive and clear on her career goals. She's successfully moved into different roles, tackling unknown territory with confidence. She has three young children at home and is debating having a fourth. Not only that, she has primary caretaking responsibility for both of her parents, who are separated, and now both living under her roof. Her husband does shift work so at times she's shouldering the load on her own. When I think I'm tired, I think of Melanie and reframe.

I was curious what kept Melanie focused on her career. How does she maintain energy for her career despite her demanding home life? It's simple, she said. She needs to keep learning and growing and stretching. Her home life is chaotic, but when she's unfulfilled at work, that's when she's really unhappy. By progressing at work, Melanie feels grounded, in control and competent. Melanie needs to feel valued and that she's making a difference and contributing to something meaningful, beyond what she gets from her home life. When she's on autopilot at work, doing the same thing over and over, she feels bored and unfulfilled. It feels like a grind. She believes she deserves more and is capable of more. She asks herself, *Why do I have to wait?* When she feels overwhelmed at home, she said she reminds herself that the dark periods are temporary and that there's a big, bright light at the end. And she knows that nobody is going to build the road for her. She knows that she has to carve the path. She fears that if she doesn't know where she's headed or move her feet continually forward, then she'll stagnate. This is what keeps her motivated and driven. Part of Melanie's vision includes a more senior leadership role and she knows she needs to continually gain varied experiences to get her there.

The meaning in Melanie's life comes from her family and from her professional aspirations. Purpose not only has been shown to help us persist through the daily grind, as Melanie does, but also is associated with lower risk of all-cause mortality. When you have a larger vision and can see it being fulfilled, you are engaged and, as it turns out, healthier too. You stick through a lot in the short term because you know the long term will be worth it.

So you can spend an hour watching *The Great British Baking Show* or scrolling aimlessly through Instagram or you can change your life. I'm not saying you have to give up all the watching and scrolling. But begin by jotting down ideas about what you're known for, what you want to be known for, what excites you, what doesn't, what impact you want to have, what influence you want to possess and what legacy you want to leave. Yeah, I know—big questions! Write until you have a statement or a paragraph or vision board that describes you living at the horizon. You can try it on, share it with others and evolve it over time. It's not about more doing, it's about more being: being your best, most fulfilled you.

From comfy in the zone to "reach, stretch, grow"

I hear too often from women that they don't feel certain enough to speak up, stick their neck out with an idea or apply for a role that they aren't already experienced at. "If I haven't done it, I'm not doing it," "If I'm not great at it, why bother?" or the perennial "I'm not ready yet." It's certainly a source of fear for a lot of us. There's comfort in staying in our lane and doing what we know. But what if you could shift your mind to stop thinking about what you don't know (yet) and get excited about what you could know (soon)? What if you could tell yourself a story about what could be gained? Certainly, most women aren't comfortable with this way of thinking (yet).

Rachel Morrison, a senior lecturer at the Auckland University of Technology, presented research at the World Economic Forum that described an interesting gender difference found while studying those who reported loving their jobs. There was a clear distinction between those who cited loving their job either due to a) feeling very capable at it, or b) being challenged to stretch their abilities. Can you guess the gender distinction she found?

Those who cited loving their jobs because it gave them a feeling of competence were almost all women. The women found satisfaction and enjoyment from a hard job well done, from using the skills and abilities they had to their fullest. The women deemed themselves a good fit for a job when their skills matched the requirements, and they could contribute meaningfully. The men, however, talked most about being tested, stretched or overcoming an insurmountable obstacle.

How would you describe the job you love or loved most? Is the reason because you are damn good at it? Did you derive satisfaction from executing on your knowledge and expertise flawlessly? If so, how long did that high last? And was it always that way? Remember when you were learning that very thing you are great at now? You likely struggled in the beginning; it was through practice and perseverance that you mastered the skill. Didn't that feel great too? We aren't born experts at anything. There is always a learning curve. What if you could shift your mindset to be ready to stretch into the unknown, instead of relying on current expertise?

This reminded me of a story I heard at a retirement party for a wise and adored female leader. As she recounted her career journey, she told us about a turning-point question her husband asked her many years ago when she was considering a new position. Her husband asked her, "Why would you ever take a job when you can already do all the responsibilities required?" What a great reframing question to make her open and brave toward new opportunities.

To reframe from being comfy in the zone to being ready to reach, stretch and grow, I advise women to shift from a development plan to an experience plan. Most people take stock at the end of the year and ask, "What do I need to develop to get better at the job I'm doing?" Maybe it's taking a course, reading some resources, meeting with a manager or mentor, etc. Contrary to what you might think, these kinds of development plans do little for your future, little to become your future ideal self, little to challenge your sense of self and build your confidence. The readiness to take on new daunting tasks, projects or roles is built over time from continual, small stretches. That builds confidence for what feels like bigger, bolder stretches.

Think instead about an experience plan. What experiences do you need to have to truly grow and develop? What seasoned stakeholders do you need to interact with, what presentations do you need to make, what meetings do you have to get into, what projects do you need to be after? How can you get real-time learning that not only helps in your current role but builds capability for future roles? How can you gain experiences that fuel a love of stretching, instead of hiding behind a book or course in a comfortable zone of incremental learning?

The more you practice being uncomfortable, the easier it will become. The more you take small leaps, the more able you will be to take larger ones. And don't wait to be asked: you go get 'em!

From bored and blocked to "unleash and unlock"

The desire to keep learning is noble but must be directed toward a clear purpose. Learning is a supercharger when it fuels your passion and moves you toward your personal vision. Until you do the think-ing on your personal vision, you are likely making unconscious decisions or, worse, no decisions at all. That's when your career is happening to you. That's when you begin to feel bored or blocked. It's time to unlock what's possible and unleash what gets you fired up.

John Coleman, one of the authors of *Passion & Purpose*, reminds us that most people don't find their passion at work. For most of us, our true purpose doesn't strike us like a bolt of lightning with a big aha. We have to build it. We have to both make our work meaning-ful and take meaning from our work. And it can change over time. Many people now have multiple careers over a lifetime or make changes for many personal reasons. That's good too. The import-ant thing is that you find a horizon and look to it. You can turn on the road, but there is always a horizon up ahead. You create that. Then you can make decisions about how to skill up, what experiences to seek, which opportunities to take and which to turn down.

Don't get stuck in shouldn'ts or won'ts. Be flexible and open. A woman once said to me that she definitely didn't want to be a VP. "I know that about myself," Carmen said. She was a senior manager vying for a director role. I know she'll move into one because she's intelligent and driven and adds value to every role she's in. Most importantly, she has created a broad network of influence across the organization already. It's really only a matter of time before she's promoted, and if she's not, her organization should worry that she will be snapped up somewhere else.

I was baffled then that Carmen was so closed off to progressing to the VP role. She expressed her desire to be closer to the action and to the people she leads. She said that the VPs in her organization were in the dark: no one gave them the straight goods and real infor-mation. She also said they really didn't do much at all. I had a good laugh at this, recalling all the meetings I'd attended and observed. Hours and hours of meetings where it did indeed feel like nothing was being done. I'm sure it looked that way to the employees who watched the countless muffins and dry sandwiches carted in and out of the conference rooms.

I assured her that I was not pushing her to continue an upward ascent by any means. But I tried to change her story about learning, stretching and growing. It was important that Carmen not close herself off to future opportunities. She may end up changing her mind; crazier things have happened. We talked about being the kind of leader who fosters open communication and information sharing. There is truth in the statement that as leaders become more senior, they can be further away from what's "happening on the ground." But it doesn't have to be that way. We talked about what doing the real work meant at different levels. While she is "closer to the action" in the day-to-day work, senior leaders are "closer to the action" on strategic work, such as understanding how to address the economic, social, political and environmental factors that impact their business.

Carmen is a great people leader and loves it. I asked if she could see herself helping other people become great people leaders. After all, when you increase your span of control, you directly manage a group of people, but you also indirectly lead an entire department. Your job then includes helping your direct reports become great people leaders. You move from coaching employees to coaching the coach. She'd never looked at it that way before. Carmen slowly became more flexible; her thinking was expanding.

It's worth noting here too that there is a big difference between a goal and a vision, but they are complementary. Jessica's story illustrates this difference well. She had a career goal of becoming an executive. She worked at a large corporation and was stymied in a small department with a horrible manager who blocked every opportunity for advancement. But Jessica stuck so rigidly to her goal of becoming an executive that she had tunnel vision. She could only see one path forward in that particular organization. She had moved across the country, uprooted her life and took a big risk to come to this company. Damn it, she was going to make it work. It became the sole focus of her development activities.

During our conversations, I asked Jessica what appealed to her about an executive role. Why did she aspire to it anyway? She talked a lot about having broader influence and impact. I was happy to hear this because executive roles are not easy and doing it solely for the money or title is a grim place to be. Over her career, Jessica had worked in many roles at organizations big and small. So when we brainstormed all the ways she could have impact, Jessica realized that her vision needed to meld her personal and professional ambitions to be truly fulfilling. She began to search for opportunities that fulfilled her, not just a chance to become an executive in her current organization. She took different meetings, picked up the phone to network with old acquaintances and sought support outside her company. She moved from chasing a role to building a life.

Within months she moved back to the other side of the country in what at first seemed like a lateral move, but it had potential for tremendous influence in her industry as a whole. Her former organization was still in that role's purview, and now it seemed so small in comparison to the impact she could have in her new job. And because she's a rock star, she was offered an executive position shortly after her arrival. She achieved her goal of becoming an executive. But if she hadn't broadened her vision of what was possible, what kind of leader she wanted to be and how she wanted to contribute, she may not have seen or seized this opportunity. She might still be stuck. The vision broadened her horizons and gave her a life, a location and a community that she'll continue to build out over the long term.

Don't stop at the desire to keep learning. Aim that learning toward your horizon. You can always change your mind or redirect your efforts along the way. Your learning will never be wasted, but at least you can make it extremely purposeful. Don't just tell your manager you want to keep learning and growing. Tell them how, where and for what purpose. Link it to a broader vision and longer-term purpose so that when you go through your days, you keep an eye on the horizon.

If you shape your future, you will not have to look back and wonder what more you could have accomplished if you had used those days and weeks differently. Look up from the torrent of today and look out to tomorrow. Create a personal vision and be flexible and open to opportunities. Take small, deliberate steps to get you there. And remember, it's not about *doing* more, it's about *being* more for yourself.

1:1:1 Plan

Once a week

- **Recall and reinforce.** Keep your vision top of mind as you progress through your day and your week. Consciously consider it before you say yes or no to something, or use it to guide another decision. Feel great about your vision. If you don't, change it.

- **Fish for self.** Release selfish and cast your own net instead. Do one thing each week that is 100 percent completely for you. Maybe it's a quiet coffee alone, reading a book just for fun or going for a walk or workout. Maybe it's journaling or knitting or connecting with a friend. It can be anything, but it has to be your choice, something you enjoy that's just for you. Look up from the day-to-day grind and build a habit of doing something for yourself that impacts you longer term. It may feel like a frivolous activity, but a habit of self-care and compassion will feed your ability to dream, think bigger and create the life you want.

- **Audit time sucks.** Review your calendar. Determine what you did that moved you toward your vision, even if only a teeny tiny bit. When did you consciously make a decision that was guided by your vision? What sucked up your precious time? Audit and adjust.

Once a month

- **Embrace novelty.** Do one thing that you think you can't, won't or don't do. Eat a new food; read something different; engage in a different activity; have a different conversation. Show yourself it's not that bad. Show yourself it can be fun. Build up to riskier and riskier things (while still remaining safe).

- **Revisit ruts.** Identify if you fell into a rut this month. If you did, what was it? Make a conscious decision to get out of it.

- **Pinpoint a model.** Think about a role model you admire for their ability to articulate a vision and progress toward it. Choose someone who is inspiring to you because they found ways to believe in their potential despite obstacles. This person could be known to you or unknown, famous or not, living or deceased; it doesn't matter. Find learnings, tips, strategies or mindsets you can use in your own journey. Put a few into practice.

Once a year

- **Evolve your vision.** Reflect on your personal vision statement, paragraph or vision board at the end of the calendar year or your organization's fiscal year. What movement have you made? Where would you like to make more movement? Determine if your vision needs to evolve and be okay with the fact that you want to change it. Recall times when you felt like you were aligned with your vision. How did it feel and what were you doing? Determine where to focus your energy and efforts now.

- **Unlock learnings.** Make a learning list that captures what you have learned over the last several years. Capture your learned skills, capabilities, knowledge and mental shifts. Which learnings do you use? Which are underused and could be applied further? Next, capture new things you'd like to learn. What experiences can you have to gain these learnings?

- **Build support.** Create a group of people that help you toward your vision. Sometimes this is referred to as a career board, advisory panel or your posse of people who will both support you and challenge you. This combination of professional and personal contacts will give you what you need when you need it.

Sometimes it's deep reflection, sometimes it's a much-needed laugh and sometimes it's a loving nudge in the right direction. We need these people to support us, build our confidence, challenge us and act as our advocates. Going it alone is needless, and it sucks.

Which reframe was most useful for you in this chapter on looking up and out to the horizon?

From _____ to _____ .

3

DO
LESS
SHIT

From "I get a shitload done" to **"I gotta do less shit"**

WE SAT IN a taxi together on the way to the airport. Anna was a participant in a leadership program I had just led for her company. We were both worn out from a long week of introspection, learning, dinners, networking . . . all amid monitoring emails and fires back in the office and on the home front. You know the drill. Anna said she wanted to make a quick call home en route.

I couldn't understand what Anna was saying because she was speaking in her native Eastern European language, but I knew she was speaking to a young child and then to an adult. When she got off the phone, I commented how hard it is to be away from family for a week. She told me that she was a single mother to a young boy. I knew how tirelessly she worked at the office and at home. I got the distinct feeling that her day never ended.

It was then that Anna told me her team had staged an intervention before she came to this workshop. Her team, composed of men, came into her office all at once and asked to speak with her. They reminded Anna that the company saw something in her; that she had potential to rise to more senior levels in the organization. They respected her immensely and told her that she didn't have to take on every challenge herself, she didn't need to stay up late into the night sending emails and she didn't need to double-check everything they did. They wanted Anna to delegate more responsibility to them so they could support all that she was trying to do. They were ready to be the team that she needed. Anna needed to let go and focus on more strategic things. And then the real crusher came: they told Anna that she wasn't being a good role model to her team or to her son. Clunk, did your heart just fall into your gut too? I know. That was one piece of tough love.

Anna believed that she needed to add value on everything, everywhere, at every moment. She was sucked into an endless tactical vortex that left her spinning, dizzy and exhausted. The reality is you can't add value on everything. It's simply not possible, and it's not desirable.

Early in my career I engaged in a 360-degree assessment. A 360 is a joyous form of feedback in which your skills, effectiveness and influence as a leader is evaluated by everyone. Direct reports, colleagues and your manager; everybody has input! Sarcasm aside, it's full of affirming, surprising and at times troubling feedback. It's horrible-tasting medicine, but it works. For me, it was the catalyst I needed to propel my career. Feedback from the various stakeholders told me that I was perceived as more tactical than strategic.

At first, I was confused: I knew business; I'd gone to business school. I built strategy and a business. I could make cognitive connections between disparate pieces of information and make sense of trends and their implications. I built programs that taught other leaders to be strategic! How was this possible? Then I realized that no one had visibility on my strategic capabilities. More importantly, I was too weighed down in execution to devote time to strategic activities. I had to change what I was known for if I wanted to progress further in my organization.

After I received my 360 results, I sought to understand more about what it meant to be strategic. I also wanted to know how to be *perceived* as strategic. As I became embroiled in research, I quickly came across some shocking and disheartening data. I found a study stating that strategic ability was, in fact, women's Achilles' heel. Not a great start. While at first I was kind of glad that I wasn't the lone woman struggling in the weeds, maybe that would have been better for all of us. I would have taken one for the team if I could, I swear, but unfortunately strategic ability, or being perceived as strategic, seems to be a challenge for many women.

Herminia Ibarra and Otilia Obodaru studied thousands of 360 assessments from INSEAD's renowned executive education program and found that women outshone men in all of the leadership dimensions measured, except one—envisioning. They defined the ability to envision as sensing opportunities and threats in the environment, setting strategic direction and inspiring constituents in execution. They also offered three explanations for why women might be "vision-impaired." First, some women don't put as much stock into visioning activities as men do. It's not seen as a valuable way to spend one's time. Second, some women lack the confidence to go out on a limb with an untested idea. I've seen this firsthand. Third, some women are skilled at strategic visioning but do so in such a collaborative manner that they don't get credit for it. Hmm, they may be onto something here.

The quest to be perceived as strategic may in fact be a harder battle for women than men. Why is that? Is it because women take on more and bask in the multitask? Well, yes. Is it because men feel less guilty delegating? Maybe. Is it because men are smarter than women? Gosh, *no*! By reading research and working with hundreds of women, I've learned the common patterns that explain the tactical rut:

- executing with excessive pride ✓
- hanging on to too much work ✓
- making ourselves subservient ✓

"Give it to me; I'll get it done"

You likely have an endless to-do list distracting you from important strategic priorities. You love ticking off the quick but unimportant task. You relish the act of drawing that check mark. Admit it. You likely also spend more time in reactive mode than in reflective mode, don't you? You delight in your ability to get a shitload done. "Give it to me; I'll take care of it!" you say.

Add to this your ability to multitask at work and at home. It's your superpower, right? It's a source of pride for women. How else can you keep all those balls in the air, all those precarious plates spinning? Pick whatever metaphor you like; it doesn't change the fact that multitasking does more harm than good. Multitasking leads to less productivity, poor quality of performance and diminished psychological well-being. It causes you to become distracted and overwhelmed. It reinforces the frenzy of being tactical and can make you appear scattered in your communications. None of this supports perceptions of strategic capability.

Related to this is an addiction to being busy. Think about it. In the modern workplace, busyness is related to influence and importance; it's how we convince ourselves that we are useful and valuable. Those who work efficiently or have time on their hands are viewed as lazy, self-centered or not as driven. Yet this busyness distracts from what's truly important and causes exhaustion, overwhelm and a myriad of health implications. When was the last time you said to yourself, "I'm hanging on by a thread" or "I'm barely keeping afloat" or "Is this really worth it?"

The problem with focusing excessively on execution, basking in busyness or multitasking like mad is that you get trapped in the hamster wheel of tactical work and that's all you are known for. Executing, not leading. Tactical, not strategic.

What are you known for in your organization? What would your boss or other senior leaders say about you? Are you known for getting things done, executing with excellence, managing projects on time and on budget? Or would they describe you as a long-term thinker, solving the vexing problem at hand, being on top of big trends and problems before they come to a head?

Being good at executing your responsibilities is critical. We rise through organizations based on our expertise and ability to deliver. To a point. This is where the typical manager tops out. If you have aspirations to take on more complex roles or projects, you have to get known as someone who has ideas, navigates complex problems, plans amid complexity and influences key stakeholders. You must get known as strategic.

The leaders I work with express it as "wanting to make a shift in how they're known in the organization." They want to move from being known as a "go to" on executing in a particular area of expertise to being a "go to" for solving emerging issues. They realize they need to get out of the daily grind so they can focus on the future and more strategic issues.

You may ask why being perceived as strategic is important. You may even be saying, "I don't want to move into senior roles in my organization. I'm good where I am, thank you very much." It doesn't matter. Organizations today expect all employees to be more strategic: to think beyond the immediate, anticipate challenges, make connections between courses of action and their impact on people and plans. Then if you do wish to progress into more senior positions, you must create and translate strategy, prioritize focus and plan the work of a team or function, review work and ensure quality, develop future leaders and successors and manage complex change.

As one female senior leader at an insurance company said to me, "It's a deal breaker if the executives in my organization don't see me as strategic. I won't progress any further." Similarly, a junior analyst said during a strategic workshop, "Now I see why I can't get people to listen to me. I'm too tactical. I need to show how this links to our broader goals." No matter what your role, what industry you work in or what goals you have for your career, thinking and communicating with a strategic lens will serve you well.

"It's better if I just do it myself"

Studies have shown men to be more comfortable with delegation, or off-loading tasks. Women tend to take control of tasks and care more about how and when something gets done and to what level of quality. Also, empathy comes into play more with women: "That person is too busy, so I will just do it."

Modupe Akinola, Ashley E. Martin and Katherine W. Phillips published a paper in the *Academy of Management Journal* that reports on the results of five research studies exploring gender differences in delegation. They found that female leaders were less likely than male leaders to leverage the benefits that delegation can bring.

They state that delegation benefits the self (the leader) and therefore is an assertive act, and it also benefits others (individuals and teams) and therefore is a communal act as well.

They found that female leaders, as compared to male leaders, have more negative associations with delegating and feel greater guilt about delegating than men. Women see delegation as self-serving more than as communal. These associations result in women delegating less than men; when they do delegate, they have lower-quality interactions with subordinates.

Be honest: are you doing the work of one or two levels below you? Do you believe it's faster to just do the work yourself rather than fixing all the mistakes a subordinate or colleague would make? Do you strive for perfection and fail to distinguish when good is good enough? Are you reluctant to ask for help at work or at home? All of this keeps you bogged down, leaving little time to lift your head to the horizon. It keeps you in reactive mode instead of in strategic reflective mode. It also robs others of personal growth and development.

Recall Anna's team from the opening story in this chapter. Her team wasn't just looking out for her, they were looking out for themselves too. Have you worked for a boss who won't delegate anything? Worse yet, have you worked for a manager who constantly looks over your shoulder checking every minute detail? The former breeds boredom and the latter irritation. When a leader believes they must add value on everything, they deprive others from adding their full value, or from learning how they can be more valuable to the team and the organization. If you can't delegate and grow others in the process, you will not be seen as leadership material.

"I'm being a good team player"

I was leading a lively conversation with senior HR leaders in San Francisco on the common barriers women face—in particular when they're assessed on their potential to move up the ladder. One of these barriers was described as being trapped on the hamster wheel of tactical work. At this point, a male leader commented that he's observed this phenomenon in his own organization. In fact, he pointed to a recurring theme on his own team, which consists of both men and women. He noticed that at the end of every meeting, the female peers took all the action items. In addition to the follow-up work, they also got stuck with the administrative details and cleaning up the cups and debris in the meeting room. Essentially, they bore the brunt of the grunt work. "It happens all the time!" the leader said.

The phenomenon the leader described above is so common it's been given a name: office housework. It's the set of tasks that need to be done but are underappreciated and unpromotable. Research from Laurie Weingart, senior associate dean of education at Carnegie Mellon University's Tepper School of Business, found that on average women spend five hours per week on office housekeeping tasks not directly related to their jobs. That's over two hundred hours a year!

Do you say yes to low-visibility projects or committees, take on routine work that requires little skill, plan parties or lunches, take notes furiously, organize repeatedly, set up for meetings, clean up after meetings and on and on and on? Ask yourself, Do these tasks help me get promoted? A raise? Even a thank-you? If someone told you that you had two hundred extra hours to work on your existing role, make more sales, create a process, develop a new skill or maybe get more sleep or exercise, would you take them? Of course you would. So do it. Take the time back.

Whether it's making yourself feel lesser than by taking on too many menial tasks, you may be perpetuating a cycle of subservience. Women are socialized to pitch in and care for others as young girls. We grow up to believe that a good team player pitches in and helps. A good team player says yes, not no. This is a nice philosophy for all humans to live by, for sure. The problem is that women get saddled with this version of team playing too often and the implications are dire.

"You don't build the life you want by saving time. You build the life you want, and then time saves itself. Recognizing that is what makes success possible."

LAURA VANDERKAM

If you feel undervalued at work, or that you could be doing more, or that the organization is wasting your talents, it takes its toll on your engagement. Picking up grunt work while others work on high-profile projects makes your effort seem futile. If you're not using your talents to their fullest, if you're not learning and growing or you have no influence, you're likely to feel resentful and it's time to change how you're spending your work hours. In the words of Dolly Parton, "If you don't like the road you're walking, start paving another one." Sing it, sister! And Dolly knows a thing or two about working nine to five.

As you know, when you spread yourself too thin by taking on too much, at some point things begin to slide at work, home or both. It's a slippery slope that puts you in a worse position. You're exhausted constantly, and that affects your work and your relationships. You think you're getting ahead, but at what cost? You risk burnout, and a sick and unhealthy you is no good to anyone.

Think about how you define *team* when you decide to pitch in. By taking one for the team or by saying yes to non-promotable tasks, are you taking time away from more strategic tasks? The answer is likely yes. When you say yes to something, you are by default saying no to something else. Or you're working around the clock to get it all done, which isn't sustainable either. Remind yourself of your core team responsibilities and focus on those first. Then if you have more time and energy to give, focus on visible tasks important to your organization's strategy and its leaders. That's how you'll stay sane—and how you'll get ahead.

Activity: Your strategic story

It's a good time to pause and reflect on how much you tend toward the tactical or the strategic. Does your mindset keep you in the weeds or above the waterline? Do your behaviors tend to be reactive or reflective? Read the following statements and check off those that are mostly true for you.

- [ ] I tell myself I couldn't possibly take on something new because I'm way too busy already.

- [ ] My long to-do lists run my life.

- [ ] I constantly tell myself and others how busy I am.

- [ ] I find it easier to do things myself.

- [ ] I have a hard time saying no when asked to take something on.

- [ ] I find it hard to let go of control of tasks at home and work.

- [ ] I spend more time reacting to what comes my way than reflecting on strategic priorities.

- [ ] I believe that multitasking is my superpower.

- [ ] I feel guilt when asking others to take on work.

Look at the statements you checked off to be mostly true and reflect on the following questions.

How do these statements make you feel? Do your mindsets and actions help create order and priority, or are they causing freneticism and chaos?

_____

_____

_____

_____

Which statement causes you the most trouble? What new story do you need to start telling yourself?

_____

_____

_____

_____

Reframes
. . . .

I believe you have good intentions for wanting to get a lot done. You want to be a great worker and accomplish a lot. You want to be accomplished in your personal life too. But now is the time to ask yourself, Am I getting the right things done? Will I be more successful, happier and more rested if I can triage, say no once in a while and cut myself some slack? Can I become a master at making strategic choices instead of being caught in tactical execution? Yes, you can. Now read on for important reframes you may need to make.

From multitask madness to "strategic badass"
. . . .

Get it through your head: you can't and won't get everything done. Harsh, I know, yet true. Believe me, I remember the glory days early in my career. They were simpler times. You couldn't check email at home, texting didn't exist and no one would call you at home. I headed to work, checked off my to-do list and went on my way. No children, no pets. Ah, the simplicity of it all. Wow, I sound old.

Today we are reachable all the time; we can't disconnect. Well, we can, but we don't. And when you are in a role that requires overseeing the work of others and managing constant change or involves different time zones, there is a relentless feeling of never being done. But that doesn't mean you have to get sucked into a vortex of anxiety and dread of never-ending work.

I was leading a group of aspiring female executives at a professional services firm through a live networking exercise. The women were practicing their introductions to one another. As I walked around and listened to the small talk, I noticed a distinct pattern. The answer to the questions "How are you?" or "What are you up to these days?" was invariably a single word: "Busy." Listen for it. It's everywhere. I bet you say it all the time. We all do. And the reality is you are busy. Everyone is. Ask a retired person; they're busy too.

But *busy* enables excuses. It prevents us from tackling what's important and meaningful at work and in our lives. And it doesn't help build your profile because a generic answer of "busy" doesn't tell people the important things you're working on, your successes or your impact.

I once had a boss who banned the word *busy* from our vocabulary at work. He wasn't being insensitive; he wanted to help us. He knew we were all busy. He wanted us to get better at talking about our workloads, at prioritizing and reprioritizing, at raising our hand sooner when things felt out of control. He wanted to shift the culture from "being busy" to "adding the most important value." He wanted to ensure the most important strategic goals were advancing. Banning *busy* gave power back to the employees to have conversations about what could get done by when.

You are busy. You will always be busy. Try to replace it with thinking, *What is the most important thing I must do right now?* Ask yourself if it's the strategic thing to do.

Maybe you will choose to sit at your desk for hours on end risking a stiff neck and sore back because if you finish that report today, it will allow you more thinking time tomorrow as you plan a presentation. Maybe you will choose to stop working on the report for a few hours to meet with a colleague over lunch because you need to prioritize strategic networking for an upcoming job opportunity. Either way, you make a purposeful choice.

Every day requires fierce prioritization in a way that it didn't require in the past. You need to set strategic priorities, carve out milestones and live with the fact that some things can't get done. Then you need to communicate your focus to your manager, get feedback and readjust if necessary. Don't wait until you're at a breaking point. Don't get sucked into the whirlwind of busy. Make strategic choices to add value and advance bigger goals. The rest will have to wait. But, but, but. Something will always be waiting in the wings. Always. Make sure it's not your opportunities or what keeps you happy and healthy.

From determined to hold on to "happy to hand over"

I've never heard anyone say that they enjoy sleepless nights. I've never heard anyone relish doing everything themselves at work with no help from anyone. So why do we continue to try to do it all?

You do it for good reasons with good intent. You want good outcomes; you want everything to go perfectly; you want to protect yourself and others from failure. It feels good to be needed and relevant. But you know what I'm going to say, don't you? Doing it all creates stress and it creates reliance. You need to be needed on relevant strategic tasks, not those tasks that keep you in the weeds. Doing it all creates a vicious cycle that gets harder and harder to break.

If you struggle with delegation, determine if you have the team you need to let go. Focus your time on coaching and development and replacing skill sets if required. It will be a ton of work to get over the hump, but the benefits are priceless. You can do your job well when your team is humming along the majority of the time. You can't be considered for strategic projects or new roles if you're always in the weeds. Find a way to prioritize delegation.

If you struggle with guilt when assigning work, try reframing how you see delegation by emphasizing the communal nature of it. Not only can your team members learn new skills and responsibilities, but you can also add more value to the team and the organization when you spend time on future-focused issues.

Remember Anna from the opening story of this chapter? After her "intervention," Anna realized that she needed to let go and delegate to her team. It didn't mean she was failing: it meant she was succeeding. But she couldn't shake the feeling that delegating was a way to get rid of the trivial or less important work. She couldn't see how that would aid in the growth of her team.

Sometimes delegation is viewed as the manager's dumping ground. This is where you play a huge role in positioning seemingly undesirable work. When I was looking at what work I could delegate to one of my team members, I easily identified a project-tracking spreadsheet. (Yes, this was before the wonderful software that exists today that makes this job more efficient.) At first, I felt guilty about pushing down this administrative task. I knew I needed to reframe how I was thinking about it. I asked myself, *Who was closer to the project details: the team or me?* The team, of course. *Where is my time better spent: in the weeds or strategic oversight and planning?* The latter, of course.

Next—and this is the most important part—I made sure that the task acted as a catalyst for learning, not as a mere exercise of updating a spreadsheet. I sat down periodically with the individual and reviewed the project list. I asked the person to do some analysis and come prepared with their thinking on critical issues, such as: how many projects each team member was leading; which were profitable and why; which were more labor intensive and why; which projects might we say no to in the future and why. I asked for her recommendations on processes, roles and resource requirements. I was stretching her strategic thinking skills. The spreadsheet wasn't just a pesky list: it was the data source for important planning and budget decisions. When you frame it right, delegation isn't a selfish act; it's critical for growth and development and it's good business.

Some of you may work with others who don't report to you but you need to ensure that tasks are delegated and completed. Sara was in that position frequently. She was new to her role as a department VP. She was an experienced leader, forthright and assured. In preparation for her first big client proposal at this new company, she partnered with Mark, a male colleague from sales who had been with the organization a long time. Normally a sales team member would quarterback the sale, own the proposal and draw on assistance from experts as required. Sara and her team members were the content experts in this situation. Because Sara was new, her intention for the meeting was to find out how the process worked and who she could allocate on her team to work with Mark.

The meeting didn't turn out at all like she expected. In his usual style, Mark arrived at the meeting with no notebook or pen, conveniently rendering him unable to capture information. He volunteered no time to write the proposal or lead next steps. He simply relayed information to Sara and left. Despite being two levels above

Mark, Sara left feeling like she reported to him. Worse, she left with all the action items and little support for the sale.

Sara wanted to make a good first impression and was fearful of stepping into her leadership at this early juncture. She was afraid to delegate to Mark and hold him accountable. Sara let a fear of not being liked turn into a whole lot of work. She let her status of being new and not knowing yet how things worked distract her with tasks that weren't directly hers. She made herself subservient even when she was the one with greater formal authority. She learned later that Mark had a track record of getting others to do the lion's share of work while he sat back to collect the sales credits. Lesson learned. She knew she wouldn't let that cycle continue. She called another meeting with Mark and clarified how things would go from that moment on, respectfully but firmly. She outlined roles and delegated tasks to Mark and to her team. She took less shit so she could do less shit.

From voluntold to "be bold"

Office housework is one way we sign up to be a good team player and make ourselves subservient. Many of us don't realize we're stuck in what can become a vicious cycle of volunteering or being voluntold for nonstrategic tasks. It is so pervasive.

Heidi worked on a team of creatives—she was the only woman alongside three men—who had frequent brainstorm meetings. She realized after reading my LinkedIn post "To Get Ahead, You Can't Be the Brunt of the Grunt Work" that she was creating a vicious cycle for herself. She had unwittingly fallen into the role of notetaker and she realized she may no longer be viewed as an equal. She feared that her team and maybe even her boss saw her more as the admin rather than an equal creative force. She was determined to change it.

The very next meeting, the pattern predictably continued. As she sat down, a team member immediately rolled the flip chart marker to her, proclaiming, "Here you go." But that day, instead of standing up at the flip chart and recording the brainstorm, she rolled the marker back to the center of the table and said, "I've been at this for a while now. How about someone else have a go?" The three men just stared at her silently for what felt like an eternity to Heidi. But sure enough, after what was likely only a few seconds, someone picked up the marker and said, "I'll do it." "Way to go, Heidi!" is what I wrote back to her after reading her story.

Did Heidi's colleagues force her to take notes? No, they didn't. They didn't even ask her the first time. Heidi thought she was being a good team player. She may have even believed she was exercising leadership by volunteering that first time. Instead, she ended up becoming subservient. You don't get noticed by capturing other people's ideas; you get noticed by contributing to the conversation, having great ideas, challenging ideas, making ideas better and explaining those ideas to people who matter. Those are the activities that count for performance reviews, salary negotiations and promotions.

Escaping the subservient team player trap requires that you work on strategic tasks a fair amount of time. This requires that you say no. A lot more than you likely feel comfortable with now. Stephen Covey, author of the classic book *The 7 Habits of Highly Effective People*, said, "You have to decide what your highest priorities are and have the courage—pleasantly, smilingly, unapologetically—to say no to other things. And the way to do that is by having a bigger 'yes' burning inside."

I like this notion of a burning yes. It's better than the heartburn and the burning ulcer you have from trying to do everything. You need to get clear on what your burning yesses are. These are your strategic priorities at work and at home.

When I talk to women about taking on new work, a different role or a promotion, the common reaction is "I ain't got time for that" or "I don't want that headache." Most are barely surviving in their current role. With so much on their plate at home and at work, they can't fathom taking on more.

Of course, if you advance, there will be an increase in scope, risk and span of control. But the shift you need to make is knowing it's not necessarily about doing *more* stuff, it's about doing *different* stuff.

If you want to advance, you have to become masterful at skills such as building a strong team, delegating and setting boundaries.

Most women have more freedom over their calendar and increased control over where and how they spend their time once they're in senior positions. If they're doing some things right, that is. I saw this difference acutely when I moderated a panel with high-powered executives. On the panel were two women with incredibly complex executive jobs in the public eye. The first was accomplished, influential and driven. She whizzed through the questions I asked her with intelligence, humor and grace. She didn't need to rehearse her answers; they were engrained in her. Everyone wanted to be like her. This was especially true when she remarked that it was easy for her to say no. She knew she couldn't do everything and she didn't try. If she pissed someone off by saying no, then so be it. She knew it was important to keep herself healthy and balanced, as she described her passion for learning new sports over the years. She laughed as she described how she wanted to switch things up and learn how to cook new cuisines so she recently enrolled in a cooking class. She spoke of her family and all aspects of her life. She knew what was important and she focused on those things. That's what made her an utterly inspiring role model to the audience.

Contrast that with the other female executive. She appeared tense and nervous despite the pre-planning for the event she'd engaged in. Her assistant sent me a list of questions she would and would not cover. She arrived right before the panel and made us feel as though we were lucky to be getting sixty minutes of her time. She confessed on stage that she has a problem with saying no and frequently overextends herself. She made no mention of how she spends her free time. I got the inkling that she really didn't have free time or that the ways she relaxed weren't helping her.

Now, which one do you picture when you think about taking on a larger role? I'm guessing the tense, frazzled one. But it doesn't have to be that way. The first panelist was living proof of that.

Easier said than done, I know. Most of us know what we should be doing or would like to be doing. The key is to figure out the criteria for saying yes even when, and especially when, you have little time. Reasons for saying yes may be that the ask is important to customers, to the big goals or to your career because it will provide you with exposure, profile or a stretch opportunity.

Then you need to get clear on what situations make saying no strategic—for example, when it dilutes your focus, when you are unable to deliver on a promise or when it's outside the scope of your responsibility or the responsibilities you'd like to have in the future.

As you enter conversations to determine your yes or no, first off, check your own assumptions. Are you making the ask bigger in your mind than it really is? Ask to find out what is really involved. Maybe you can say yes to brainstorming ideas or advising on the process versus taking on the project entirely. Ask questions to assess the value of the work and whether your involvement would align with your goals. If you say no, provide alternatives where possible by recommending other resources to accomplish the task.

Last but certainly not least, determine what unintentional signals you are sending. Are you giving off the impression that you are always available and always willing to say yes? I remember being on vacation with my husband who was tethered to his phone and becoming increasingly agitated. He huffed and said, "Argh, why does my team keep sending me emails? You're not bothered by your team. They know I'm on vacation!" I turned to him and said point-blank, "Uh, because you're answering them."

Sometimes you must do administrative tasks, boring things or activities you've tackled what feels like a thousand times before. Sometimes there's just no avoiding it. Sometimes those tasks can act as a bit of a brain break. Maybe, just maybe, some of these activities are not so mundane after all. Perhaps these activities can be reframed into something strategic.

A former manager asked me to revamp an internal development program targeted at our future senior leaders. I was in a customer-facing role, evaluated on my ability to land big sales, launch new products and deliver solutions to clients around the world. I didn't need the distraction of a time-consuming internal project! It didn't even afford the opportunity to develop or test new content or advance any of the goals on my performance plan. But then I saw what my boss saw: a strategic opportunity. He was always thinking three steps ahead; he was good like that.

Our company had been acquired and the executive team was large, global and unknown to me—which also meant I was unknown to them. By taking on this project, I got to work directly with each member of the executive group. I had one-on-one interviews with them, facilitated a panel, guided them on assessing participants through a strategic simulation and assisted them on sharing their wisdom with the executive hopefuls on virtual webcasts. By the end, I knew them, the dynamics of the team, who the champions were and who the resisters were. They learned my capabilities and the value I brought to our clients in programs such as this one.

I also got to know the program participants—global colleagues who now could act as bridges and influencers in the markets I was trying to help. I may have run hundreds of programs like this in the past, but I realized this one was important for other strategic reasons. Originally I saw the project as a distraction to my real job, and it became one I worked hard on because it was strategic to my career.

1:1:1 Plan

Once a week

- **Banish busy.** The next time you find the word *busy* coming out of your mouth, quickly follow it up by describing a project you're working on, a challenge you're tackling or a recent accomplishment. Use phrases such as "I'm working on an interesting challenge right now," "I'm learning more about how to..." or "I'm looking forward to implementing a big win." You're busy; the person you're talking to is busy. No one is going to win the contest of being busier. Even if you are busier than the other person, that's not a prize you want to win. Start with banishing the word and then get to work focusing on the things that matter. Make your busyness purposeful and strategic, not reactive and draining.

- **Lose the pen.** Shift your contribution by showing up to a meeting with absolutely nothing but your brain. That's right: leave the notebook and pen behind. Contribute fully to the conversation. Don't panic as you feel the desperate urge to take notes. Remember, you are subtly shifting your role from notetaker to equal participant in the discussion.

- **Lift up your head.** Literally, look up. Use this as a physical reminder to get out of the weeds. Use it to remind yourself to think longer term, to see the bigger picture and to make decisions in service of what's important and strategic. Look up and take a moment to reflect. By the way, you can do this daily, not just once a week. While you're at it, turn your head left and right a few times too and release some of that tension in your neck.

Once a month

- **Study *strategic*.** Choose a person you think is strategic and observe them in meetings and other interactions. What leads you to believe they are strategic? What can you learn from them about how they prioritize, how they spend their time and how they talk about the work they do? If you want to learn more, book a chat with them and find out what techniques they use. How do they think through decisions? What criteria do they have for saying yes and no? How do they handle conversations when they are pulled in multiple directions from different stakeholders?

- **Join up.** Partner with a trusted direct report or colleague. Have the person keep you honest about how you're doing with delegation. Are you letting go, supporting team members appropriately and building skills for the long term? Remember, the investment now will pay off huge in the future.

- **Make a to-don't list.** If you are voluntold for an action item that doesn't make sense for you, say you have no bandwidth to take it on or point out that someone else's background, experience, timeframe or role would play more strongly to task. When you find yourself itching to say yes out of fear of being perceived as uncooperative or not a team player, resist the urge to comply; take a deep breath and remember why you're saying no. It's to add *more* value, not *less* value.

Once a year

- **Revisit awesome.** Congratulate yourself on a year of undertakings, results and achievements. Bask in it; you did a lot! Now consider: Were they the right things? Did they advance your professional, development and personal goals? Do you have regrets about focusing too much on some area at the expense of another? Do you have the support you need from your manager, your team and your colleagues to make strategic impact? Determine what needs to change and where you need to focus moving forward. If it helps, capture the time you spend on non-core tasks through-out the year and determine what can be deleted or minimized.

- **Recalibrate perceptions.** Talk to your manager about how they perceive you, not just your performance but your brand and strategic capability. If you want to advance or take on differ-ent or more complex work, gain their agreement on how you can focus on more strategic areas. Position your desire as add-ing more strategic value or having additional impact—versus getting rid of shit... Positioning is everything.

- **Do over and develop.** Look at the self-assessment questions in the strategic story activity (on page 77) again. Where have you made shifts in your mindset and your actions? Where must you focus now?

Which reframe was most useful for you in this chapter on becoming more strategic?

From _____ to _____ .

4

RULE THAT MEETING

From
"I show up
as usual"
to **"I'm a
standout"**

WAS DELIVERING A workshop on leadership presence at a pharmaceutical company. While the workshop was sponsored by the women's diversity and inclusion group, it was open to everyone. I'm always curious to see who turns up when it's a women-sponsored event. This time, there were thirty attendees in total—twenty-seven women and three men. My immediate reaction when I looked across the group was "These poor dudes." Jokes were thrown around about experiencing what it's like to be in the minority. I thanked the men for coming and they said it was an important topic for everyone. They were right.

After the setup and introductions, we dove into our content and discussions. About an hour into the discussion, I noticed a pattern. Every time I threw out a question, one of the men answered first. I kept a watch on my suspicions a bit longer by asking more questions and avoiding eye contact with the men. I looked beseechingly at the women—"Come on," my eyes pleaded—and yet I was met with nothing. Normally women say they are outnumbered by men and it makes them uncomfortable speaking up. But here we were, twenty-seven women and three men, and they still weren't speaking out first.

I said that before we moved on, I wanted to share an observation that was relevant to the workshop topic. I told them what I observed and that I was curious to find out what was happening. The room remained silent. The women looked surprised and somewhat guilty, and the men were shocked and sheepish. No one else had noticed that this was happening. I said we could move merrily on our way with the workshop, but it seemed pointless to talk about presence and impact in an academic sense when the real-life classroom was serving us a lesson on a silver platter.

I asked what went through each of their minds when I lobbed out a question. After some prodding, the women said, "I don't know if my answer's right" or "I don't want to sound stupid." Essentially, they didn't want to take the risk. The three men didn't see risk the same. They threw out an idea and didn't tie their answer as strongly to themselves and their worth.

Turns out communication patterns and mindset differences form early on in the classroom and persist in meeting rooms where men dominate conversations, interrupt, assert power and dismiss. Studies found that in early education, teachers call on boys more and we know from our workplace experience that leaders give more airtime to those who take it. Because the world very much still operates by male-dominated standards and rules, it causes women to hold back, to be ignored, to be talked over or to be deemed too aggressive when they do participate. This causes us to tell ourselves stories that further perpetuate the cycle. Does your brain betray you with chitter chatter about sounding dumb, with fears of being disliked or with an in-house editor who redlines your prospective comments by deeming them imperfect? It's time to tone down that chatter and let your voice break through. Let's begin with a look at the harmful stories we tell ourselves about how, when and where we can speak up. These stories come down to:

- feeling like we need to be an expert to speak up
- striving to be liked
- analyzing the perfect response

"I don't want to sound stupid"

Reams of women tell themselves they don't know enough to speak up in critical daily meetings because they aren't expert enough, experienced enough, senior enough. They don't speak from fear of sounding silly or stupid, or they don't believe they've earned the right to speak out. Or maybe they tried once, got shot down and didn't dare try it again. That's what happened to Laura.

Laura was excited when she was finally promoted from a recruiting role to business partner role with her company's sales and marketing leadership team. She was enthusiastic as she entered her first leadership team meeting, but because she was new to the role, the youngest on the team and one of the only women, she remained quieter than she normally would be. She thought it was important to listen during the early days and see how the team operated. As they were discussing an item on the agenda, Laura had an idea and decided to raise it. She actually raised her hand like a schoolchild waiting for permission to speak (oh, Laura). When acknowledged, she meekly shared her idea ending with "Have you maybe tried it this way before?"

Big, long, awkward pause. Crickets chirping. Until a senior leader spoke up and said, "Well, we don't *do* things like that around here." (Grrr, bad leader.)

Laura was mortified, embarrassed and put in her place. She began to question her suitability for the role: *Can I do this job? Am I ready? Will they ever value me? Will I get fired?* Her catastrophic thinking was out of control. It took Laura months to speak up again; every time she tried, she heard a little voice in her head: *Don't overstep; get back in your place.*

Speaking up, however, is step one. You also must pay attention to how you're breaking into the conversation. Deborah Tannen, a linguistics professor at Georgetown University, is a well-known researcher of gender communication differences. She observed that men downplay their doubt by making confident-sounding statements. Women downplay their certainty by using qualifiers and making statements sound like questions. Examples of weakening qualifiers are "Don't you think?" "If you don't mind ..." "This might be a crazy thought, but ..." "Maybe we should kinda, sorta, like ..." Women also apologize more often than men.

These qualifying statements allow our brains to remain in the fear-of-sounding-silly camp. You think you're hedging your bet when you waffle with your words. *I'll just try this sentence, test the waters*, you think. But the reality is you end up doing more damage. Say your idea with confidence; say it with conviction. I'll show you it's not safer to be a wallflower.

"I'm afraid they won't like me"

Sociologists, anthropologists and psychologists have observed American children at play and found that girls focus on building rapport through relationship while boys build rapport through status.

Tannen describes further that girls tend to play with a single best friend or in small groups. They spend a lot of time talking and use language to negotiate how close they are, how similar they are and how much they are liked. It's why only girls buy BFF necklaces, bracelets and keychains that are divided in two and shared; what at first may seem harmless and cute enforces toxic and limiting behaviors in girls. Sharing secrets is a way girls become even closer. They also learn to downplay ways one is better than the other and that sounding too sure of themselves will make them unpopular. Girls learn how to communicate in ways that balance their own needs with those of others. Keep the peace; get along; ensure everyone likes you.

Boys, by contrast, usually play in larger groups. While more boys are included in the play, not everyone is treated as equals. Boys negotiate status and accept who emerges as the leader. The boy with higher status is expected to give orders and doesn't get labeled as "bossy," like girls are. Boys use language to negotiate their status by showing off: they openly display their skill, knowledge and ability. Boys don't have to like each other to hang out.

This early conditioning with girls and boys is neither right or wrong, better or worse. They each have their upsides and their downsides. But we don't have to look too far into the boardroom to see how this plays out as adults and the disadvantages it brings to women today. Men interrupt more and battle to have their ideas heard and accepted. Men consider bringing forth contrary views by mentally calculating risks to their political capital, externalizing the outcome. They can have a good slug fest with each other and then go have a beer. They can like each other or not; it doesn't matter as much.

Women, however, may shy away from conflict and hesitate to bring up contrary viewpoints. We internalize with a fear of not being liked or respected. We take things more personally and have more difficulty working with people we don't like.

Do you have a need to keep the peace, to avoid contention or duck from conflict? Are you afraid if you say the wrong thing you won't be liked? Is it causing you to have less impact than you could? Maybe BFF lapel pins at work will solve the problem.

The reality is that by speaking out, you may in fact be disliked.

I was leading a workshop for senior female leaders at a top consulting firm. These women were brilliant and driven and still largely in the minority in a sea of men. They couldn't use the excuse that they weren't senior enough to speak out, although some still tried. We were having a conversation about barriers in their workplace when Barb said, "I have no problem saying what I think, standing up for myself or challenging others. I'm doing what I'm supposed to be doing. But I get called a bitch!"

Barb voiced what many know to be true: that women are judged more harshly when stating their opinions. They are seen as self-absorbed or bossy, while men are seen as strong and authoritative. A statement delivered by a man can be interpreted as passionate; the same statement delivered by a woman can be considered emotional, even the dreaded *hysterical*.

This is known as the assertive/aggressive stereotype and it is well researched, documented and observed. Assertiveness is valued as a leadership trait, but it is still mostly associated with men. When women act contrary to gender norms, they are penalized, which puts them in a double bind. Leadership requires assertiveness, yet women are punished when they display it. What tends to play out is that women speak up to no avail and then lose the patience and energy to keep doing so. Or they dial up the assertiveness and are labeled as aggressive.

Two researchers from Stanford University found a distinct difference when they analyzed over two hundred performance reviews from a tech company. Women received the lion's share of feedback related to communication style. And in 76 percent of women's reviews, versus 24 percent of men's reviews, there were references to being "too aggressive."

The secret sauce is the ability to flex and modulate by turning these abilities on and off at will. Women who could read the situation and strike the right balance of self-confidence and dominance with communal traits were promoted more. Are you rolling your eyes? Me too. Navigating this double bind has caused many women to throw up their hands, assume a "Why bother?" mentality and clam up.

"It has to sound perfect"

Another common reason women find it hard to break into conversations or to raise their ideas is because they're afflicted with analysis paralysis. This can play out by paying undue attention to *how* things are said or the dynamics in the room. Your ability to pay attention to the emotional cues of others and to the conflicts can be extremely useful if you're skilled at using that information to steer the group to healthy discussions. That skill is most resident, however, in facilitators, negotiators and mediators—not so much the regular meeting goer.

Often these dynamics can whip you up into a frenzy of anger, resentment, exhaustion or fear. Instead of speaking up productively and objectively, you can end up taking things personally, maybe even lashing out.

"It took me
quite a long time
to develop a voice,
and now that I
have it, I'm not
going to be silent."

MADELEINE ALBRIGHT

The other way I've noticed women overanalyze is by focusing on saying the perfect thing in the perfect way with the perfect evidence at the perfect time. Katerina was the living embodiment of this.

Katerina is an executive who strives for perfection in all aspects of her life. She pays meticulous attention to her personal appearance, she runs marathons and she always appears calm, in control and extremely articulate in her area of expertise. She came from a culture that values precision and it showed in how she executed her responsibilities. I invited Katerina and the entire executive team she was a part of to share a personal story at a leadership development program I was running for her company. I was told she probably wouldn't respond to my emails or ask any follow-up questions, but not to worry because she always showed up prepared. *Whew, one less thing to worry about*, I thought.

When the day came, I watched the members of the executive team take their seats at the front of the room and noticed that Katerina was the only one holding pages of notes. I have no problem with notes; a page of bullet points or cue cards with main messages can be helpful. But Katerina was holding pages and pages of handwritten prose that were worn and crinkled with the sweat from her palms. Sure, she was nervous, and that's okay; we can give people a pass for that, especially when what they say is authentic and from the heart. Unfortunately, that's not how Katerina came across. She was paralyzed by her desire to deliver her story perfectly. Her body was stiff and you could see the wheels turning in her head as she searched for the next line. Her speech cadence was choppy, and her eyes darted as she sought to deliver the perfect prose that lay on her lap. She didn't once look down at her notes; the pages were a security blanket in case she stumbled, which of course she wouldn't let herself do.

What saddens me is that her story was brilliant. It was hands down the most inspirational story. If you read it, you would tear up. But her desire to deliver her perfectly written story perfectly undermined her impact. Being overprepared, I would argue, undermined her passion.

Do you analyze your contribution in such excruciating detail that you end up speaking with little impact or not at all? Or do you ramble on, searching desperately for the point you're attempting to drive home? Maybe you ruminate on what you could have said after the meeting (more on this later) and berate yourself for not saying that perfect thing when you had the chance.

Activity: Your meeting story

Before we look at the reframes, let's see what mindset you're starting with when it comes to your participation in meetings.

Think of an important meeting or conversation at work you had recently that was juicy. Pick one where the content was a bit contentious or the players were interesting. In other words, don't pick a blasé, run-of-the-mill meeting. Pick one that fired you up a bit or made you nervous going in. Visualize the meeting. Now reflect on the following:

What story did you tell yourself about the meeting before you went in? (Think people, topic, context.)

_____

_____

What did you say to yourself during the meeting?

_____

_____

What story did you tell yourself after the meeting?

_____

_____

How did these stories affect your participation, your impact and the perceptions others may have of you?

_____

_____

If you could have a meeting do-over, what story would you tell yourself now?

_____

_____

Reframes

Are you sitting comfortably in the wallflower category, questioning yourself or apologizing for speaking out like others do? Are you ready to rule that meeting? Let's go!

From feeling foolish to "be fearless"

Many women tell me they limit their participation in meetings because they don't have the confidence to speak up. Often, it comes down to a mistaken belief that they have nothing to add to the conversation, that they know less than the others or that they don't have the right to speak up. Sometimes it's because they don't want to say something just to hear themselves talk. They let these fears and frustrations constrain their participation. They believe that staying silent is less of a risk. It feels like a safe alternative. But is *not* participating actually riskier?

After I gave a keynote on the ten ways women can be their own worst enemy, instead of their own best ally, a woman from the audience approached me. Carla was a senior vice president at an insurance company, and she wanted to speak about number four on the list: thinking you had to be an expert to speak up. I'd described how I see many up-and-coming and established female leaders clam up in meetings or lose confidence when speaking to senior leaders.

Carla said that when she led her own team meetings, she felt like she was on fire, full of confidence, with the ability to communicate any complex subject. But when she stepped into the management meetings where she was the only woman in the group, she didn't speak. When I confronted her about the reasons behind this, she said, "I don't know." When I probed further by asking what impact her silence was having and how she was perceived by the group, she said dejectedly, "I don't think they know how good I really am." How sad is that? My heart broke for Carla.

The irony is that she ended up giving off the exact impression she was trying to avoid: that she had nothing to say and no value to add. When you don't speak up, share your ideas or participate with impact, you risk people assuming you have little knowledge, few ideas or not enough confidence to operate at your level. Remember this too when you tell yourself that everything has already been said. You know *that* meeting, when your colleagues say the same thing over and over six ways from Sunday and the last thing you want to do is pile on just to hear yourself talk. This is what I kept telling myself for years until I received the "taking up a chair, but it's like you're not even there" feedback from a manager. While I can think of a thousand less demoralizing ways to deliver the message, I got the message loud and clear. The risk of staying silent is way higher than speaking up more.

Carla was showing her true self in her own team meetings but holding that back in meetings with peers. She realized she needed to harness the confidence she felt with her team in other settings. She needed to start telling herself a different story and always act in ways that were congruent with her true value.

How do you tame your self-limiting thoughts and avoid shutting down? Let's recall Laura, the young business partner who felt like a fish out of water with the senior sales and marketing management team. In subsequent meetings, instead of shutting down, Laura got curious. She began to ask questions and start a conversation. If someone said, "That won't work," she countered with "What is working?" "What's not working?" "What are the obstacles to trying something new?" or "What could happen if we tried it this way?"

Laura nudges herself to remember that a comment by a single person doesn't reflect the whole group's opinion. She also reminds herself that she got the job because of her creativity and ability to speak up. She was specifically told that she was a perfect fit for this team because of that. If she stopped speaking up with creative ideas, then what value was she adding?

Laura learned that every idea did not have to be a winner to be voiced. Rather than striving for perfection before speaking up, she believed that her value was in offering and collaborating. More ideas led to more discussions, which led to more solutions. Laura challenged her early belief that she had to have the same experience or background as the other team members and realized she could get involved in conversations that weren't in her domain. She rewrote her story from feeling stupid to adding value by speaking confidently and offering a different perspective. In no time, she ruled those meetings.

How do you harness a belief in yourself so that you can confidently speak out? Start by telling yourself a different story. Review and recall again your strengths, your unique value and perspective. You might not use corporate speak or have the same experience as your colleagues or your tone might be different, but all of that adds to your unique value. Remind yourself that your comments are valuable and that your perspective is needed, regardless of your position or level.

From living to be liked to "elect respect"

A successful meeting is not defined by how many people say, "Geez, she's so lovely, isn't she?" or "He really made me feel good during that conversation." If you operate under that premise, then you're likely leaving a lot unsaid. That's what happened to Irene and it almost cost her her credibility.

Irene is a senior business partner at a major bank. She is pragmatic, organized and calm. It's what makes her good at leading change projects. She's also concise, soft-spoken and reserved. You rarely see her get angry or utter profanities. She's also a self-professed conflict avoider. Irene spends her days in meetings with various stakeholders, speaking only when asked or required. It's fine by her; it's a comfortable place to be. "Do the work well and leave the talking to others" is her typical mode of operation.

One day Irene's boss gave her feedback on her communication, or lack thereof. Irene's lack of participation came off to others as a lack of urgency. People weren't confident that she really cared or was fully committed to the project. Nothing could be further from the truth, and Irene was surprised to learn that her strengths of calmness and objectivity were working against her. While Irene's character was never in question, she wasn't as respected for her skills and abilities. Irene didn't want to get in the middle of conflicts. She didn't want to be seen as taking sides or having a different point of view. She wasn't comfortable when people disagreed with her or got angry at her. She liked being liked.

Managing transformational projects, however, means navigating competing interests, resources and priorities. Irene needed to change the story she was telling herself. It wasn't her job to keep the peace; it wasn't her job to be liked. It was her responsibility to challenge ideas, to stress test options and to bring together diverse viewpoints to get to the best solutions. That's what leading change is really about.

Irene also confessed to something that I think a lot of us do. She often used introversion as a crutch. Hand up! I did it for years too. Thanks, Irene, for voicing that. Rather than speaking up proactively or speaking out with a contrary point of view, Irene fell back on the group's understanding that she was an introvert. She realized she needed to start dialing up her proactive participation in meetings. She needed to get comfortable dealing with conflict. She needed to move on from being liked to being respected for what she could bring to the table when she was fully engaged in the project discussions.

Irene elected to seek respect for what she could bring to the table. She shifted her impact in meetings by speaking up bravely more often and challenging points of view. This resulted in a shift in how others perceived her leadership. Irene was subsequently promoted and is now leading her first team. Rule those meetings, Irene!

Irene benefited with a reframe from merely showing up to standing out. She decided that it wasn't just about *what* she was doing, it was also about *how* she acted. She set goals for how she was going to show up and consequently stand out in a more positive way.

While Irene moved on from being a wallflower, recall that Barb, the senior leader from the consulting company who was called a bitch for speaking her mind, had quite the opposite problem. She was penalized for speaking up, perceived as too emotional or aggressive. Women commonly have to walk the line between appearing strong and competent but not angry. It's exhausting.

One multiyear study looked at this dynamic in 236 engineers working on project teams at a multinational software company. Over two years, the researchers analyzed more than two thousand performance ratings by supervisors, peers and collaborators. They focused on the dimensions of competence and warmth. What they found was that to be perceived as confident and influential, women must also have both competence and warmth. When raters didn't see women as warm, there was virtually no relationship between competence and confidence.

For men, warmth was irrelevant. Men had a direct relationship between confidence and competence. The more they had of one, the more they had of the other. They had more influence regardless of how liked they were. Warmth did not factor in for men.

Argh, of course, this is infuriating. We only have to look at what any female politician endures in the public eye to see what many women experience in private meetings every day. You have to be strong but not overbearing, assertive but not aggressive, warm but not too soft or akin to the office mom. It's an impossible tightrope to walk and it shouldn't be this way.

Together I believe we can change this. Thankfully, many researchers, including sociologists, behavioral economists and psychologists, are showing that the marriage of warmth and competence is the magical combination for every person, regardless of gender. Conversations on the importance of empathy and humanity in the workplace are becoming more common. We are more apt to follow, to listen, to collaborate with those we believe have our best interests at heart and who have the capability to bring those interests forward. We don't like working with bullies, jerks and those who are out for themselves. It creates toxic teams, cultures and organizations.

Rather than normalizing aggressiveness or anger across genders, I'm suggesting that we normalize warmth and competence. Many people equate warmth with being soft. What I mean by the word is not softness but empathy, understanding and listening. Like when someone gives you feedback that's hard to hear in the moment but it's the straight goods delivered in a way that is respectful and has your best interests at heart. It's strong; it's courageous—that's the warmth that we need to normalize. That's what employees and peer leaders expect today. That's what brings out the best in all of us: the ability to do our best, give our best and support others to be their best.

Here's the thing about Barb. Throughout the workshop, she was constantly on the attack; she saw everything through a negative lens; she blamed; she interrupted and spoke with an exasperated voice. No one wants to listen to anyone, regardless of gender, who acts this way. I brought up the research that humans are primarily drawn to the two capabilities of warmth and competence irrespective of gender. And yes, absolutely, women are judged more harshly on the warmth component. But isn't the way forward to create those expectations for everyone? To model the way and hold others accountable? We can do that and together change the playing field. The women agreed that would be a welcome change.

For example, when you hear people talking over one another or interrupting each other, you can say, "I observe a number of frustrated people here. We will get much further, faster if we speak one at a time and really listen to one another," or "Here are the two ideas I've heard so far; let's get back to the merits." When you hear personal attacks, you can say, "Let's agree to keep a focus on the goal and the plan, not on the person. What's the next step to solve this?" I believe it's possible to move from being liked to being respected for our strengths in empathy, connection and community by assertively speaking up; by combining warmth and strength.

From paralyzed in perfect to "prepped and present"

May is a bright and soft-spoken analyst at a large property management company. She attends many meetings where she is counted on to provide her analysis of data and trends. May told me and the other workshop attendees that she had many self-limiting thoughts. She regularly fell prey to a fear of not knowing enough, not belonging or not saying the right thing. The fear kept her stunned and numbed. She told us that she sits silently in meetings off to the side or in the back row and only answers questions that are directed at her.

But a funny thing happened. As she continued to describe these meetings, she became more and more animated. She was frustrated and clearly at a breaking point. She would watch the volley of conversation and dissect each comment, each player. She knew more about the meeting participants than they likely realized. She would marvel sometimes at their lack of knowledge and the ease with which they put themselves out there. She knew so much more than them, and she was angry at herself for not speaking out. She had rich insights to share, so why couldn't she do it?

While May appeared silent to others, she was having a robust monologue with herself every meeting. The rich discussion in her own mind went something like this:

Okay, this time I'm going to speak up more! Today's the day, May.

Yeah, of course, he spoke first. He always does.

Wow, this got heated fast.

No one is thinking about this the way I am. I'm not going against Bob and the others. That's for sure. I don't do that.

Why does Bob always interrupt like that?

Finally, someone agrees with me!

Ugh! He just said what I wanted to say.

Geez, this group seems to know much more than I thought about this.

My colleagues are so extroverted and comfortable sharing what they think. I wish I could.

This is so boring. I'm starving. What time is it?

I really should say something, but what value does my opinion have now? Everything's been said already. I don't want to repeat myself like Joe does. People will think I just want to hear myself talk. That's so annoying.

I think they're wondering why I haven't spoken. Is my face turning red? Is the boss looking at me? Now there's pressure to say something really smart.

I have nothing to say!

I'm such a loser. The meeting is over, and I didn't speak up at all.

I'm horrible in meetings.

Does any of May's internal monologue sound familiar to you? May needed to stop the damaging script in her head and move from analysis paralysis to active engagement. She benefited first from changing the story she told herself about having to say the perfect thing. Next, she learned to identify the triggers and trip-wires in real time during meetings, the moments she overanalyzed or turned sour. May's triggers are the comments made by her colleagues that riled her up; they caused an emotional reaction that she didn't like. When Bob said what she had been thinking, she got angry that she hadn't said it first; when Sheila said an idea wouldn't work, she became anxious that the project would stall. The tripwires were the items that sent her into a negative downward spiral. Paying attention to these moments makes it possible to catch yourself and reframe.

Read May's internal monologue again and see if you can identify the traps in her thinking, the triggers that send her in a downward spiral or paralyze her from speaking up. Go ahead, reread it; I'll wait.

Welcome back. Here are a few examples.

Trap: No one is thinking about this the same way I am.

Reframe: *Surely, someone else feels uneasy about this approach too. If I raise my thoughts, I am paving the way for others to speak up. We need to avoid groupthink. I can end with "Are others feeling reservations about this approach?"*

Trap: Why does Bob always interrupt like that?

Reframe: *I have an opportunity to help out others by saying, "Bob, I'd like Sheila to finish her thoughts. She has a good idea and we should hear all of it."*

Trap: Ugh! He just said what I wanted to say.

Reframe: *Okay, I know to speak up next time and that someone likely has the same thought as me. So, what's my next action here? I can say out loud, "I agree with you and here's why" or "Yes, I was thinking the same and would further the idea with this…"*

You might be thinking, *How on earth am I supposed to be in the meeting, pay attention and have this entire conversation with myself?* Well, guess what, it takes mere seconds to pay attention to your inner thoughts. You're already having a conversation with yourself anyway. I recommend that you quiet the negative tripwires by quickly reframing them. Replace the pessimistic and depressing with positive and directive. Move from "Joe knows more" to "Oops, no, he doesn't. I've done way more work in this area" and share what you've learned. Reframe from "I have to say something awesome to be worthy" to "Quiet down, brain." Say aloud, "I agree with the thoughts thus far and would add that we consider the communication strategy to the various stakeholders..." or "I agree with Joe on this point and would add a counter thought to consider..." Then hand Joe a BFF bracelet and rule the next meeting you're off to.

Once May realized she would have more success with an empowering mindset and by taming the inner talk track of assumptions, judgments and self-limiting statements, she was ready to focus on preparing her words and actions to match. She didn't have to say things perfectly; she just needed a little preparation and to be present. Here are some ways we discussed doing that.

- **Have a plan.** Know the purpose of the meeting and be clear on the agenda in advance. If you don't have it, then ask what will be covered. Know your point of view on the topics before you head in. Remember to focus both on *what* you will do and say and *how* you will show up.

- **Take up space.** Sit up tall in the middle of the group, not off to the side. I'm five foot two so I always crank the seat up to the highest setting, even if my feet dangle. Take up space by spreading things out on the table. If you are meeting virtually, ensure your face isn't the size of a pin on screen, and don't lean back in your chair. Visually signal you are there as an equal.

- **Speak up early and often.** Write down bullet points or notes in advance and during the meeting that can help you raise your viewpoint. Use concise statements and speak objectively; don't ramble on.

- **Raise your voice.** Speak at a volume so others don't have to strain to hear you and that commands attention, and be sure you're using body language that matches your confident tone.

- **Turbo-charge questions.** Questions can become a crutch for women and make you appear less knowledgeable. You can't stay in learning mode forever; you need to assert yourself. A way to combat that is to ask strategic questions that show you understand connection and impact. Rather than asking, "What is the benefit?" ask, "What would the benefits be to the variety of stakeholders with competing priorities?"

- **Know your lines.** Have a number of ready-to-go phrases, which I call back-pocket phrases, such as "I've been thinking about this differently," "What's increasingly clear to me is..." and "I'd like to go back to what she said earlier." Pull these out to initiate or break into conversations.

- **Summarize and synthesize.** If the meeting is going off track, be the one to bring it back. Summarize where things are at or ask what next steps are needed to make the ideas happen.

- **Stand your ground.** If you're interrupted, put out your hand and state that you'd like to finish. If someone said your idea first, then acknowledge that you share that position and build on it.

The last thing May did was create a mantra: a positive word, phrase or quote you say over and over to provide motivation, encouragement or focus. A mantra strengthens self-belief in situations where you feel underconfident or fearful, and a mantra keeps you on track whether you face familiar or new situations. In fact, I have written all the reframes in this book as mantras, the reframe that opens each chapter as well as the three reframes within each chapter. The chapter titles are mantras you can say to yourself too. If these short statements work for you, feel free to use them.

May's mantra was "Speak up; go for it!" and as she said it to the workshop group, she raised her hand in a fist pump. It may seem simple or silly to you, but it meant everything to May. It made her feel powerful and she knew she could say it to herself as many times as she needed to egg herself on. May went from being angry at herself and others, alienated, marginalized and powerless to revved up and ready. She was desperate to change her participation and to add value. She was excited at the possibility and at the same time terrified. But she fundamentally believed, *Today is the day, May!* She was prepped, present and supported to make change.

She realized that the discomfort she felt in speaking out was outweighed by the discomfort of seeing others get more profile, more accolades and more opportunities. She was tired of not showing her true value. She was ready to shift her impact and rule that meeting. Are you?

1:1:1 Plan

Once a week

- **Peer inside.** Observe your inner monologue while in a meeting. Identify when you make a snap judgment, when you assume or when you have self-limiting thoughts. Identify when you are tripped up by one of your own triggers and reframe it with positive thoughts. Train your brain to stay in a positive, productive and participative mindset.

- **Master the non-verbal.** Plan to signal to yourself and others that you are an equal force in the discussion. Put your chair on the highest setting or sit up tall. Be well framed on camera for virtual meetings. The goal is to make yourself more expansive. Project your voice, look people in the eye (or directly in the camera) and use strong gestures to maintain focus on you.

- **Create a to-be list.** You are all too familiar with to-do lists. A to-be list outlines how you will show up in your meetings. *In today's meeting, I will be strong, connected and credible* or *I will be positive, patient and engaged.* Use the words that you need to drive your behavior in that meeting. So when Bob interrupts again, you can say to yourself, *Be patient,* and then say out loud, "Bob, hang on and let him finish. I'm hanging on a thread here waiting to see how this ends."

Once a month

- **Fuel your power.** Reflect on your unique value add. What perspective, insights or knowledge do you have? Is your approach and style an asset? Think of your strengths, skills, abilities and characteristics. Together they form your unique value. Repeat your value add to yourself before, during and after a meeting. Use it to propel you to speak up and out more when you're silent, having an emotional reaction or worrying about being liked.

- **Shift your words.** Play with communicating more or less assertively by powering up or down your word choice. If you want to assert more strength use phrases such as "I strongly suggest," "That is absolutely right and here's why," "I agree completely and add these points," "Here is my plan to move forward." If you need to portray more warmth, then try "How about we consider," "I tend to agree and would add," "Maybe we can try" or "One thought is..." Remember the vast majority of women likely need to dial up the powerful language, not down.

- **Find a buddy.** Engage with a trusted colleague to be your profile raiser and feedback partner. Plan how to bring your voice into the room. Conspire to ensure you say ideas first. Then your partner can follow up and say things like, "I absolutely agree with you. I had been thinking along similar lines myself." Build on one another's ideas. Give each other credit throughout the meeting by repeating each other's names. Together, raise your impact and profile. I've done this and it really works. Thank you, buddy.

Once a year

- **Seek feedback.** Have a discussion with your manager and/or other colleagues. Ask how you are perceived in meetings ("How would you describe my contribution?"). Probe for perceptions about your presence ("What is one thing getting in my way?"), your value ("How would you describe the value I add to the team?") and your communication style ("What impact does my communication style have?"). What do you agree with? What is surprising? What is concerning? Determine what shifts you wish to make, and what further conversations you need to have.

- **Get specific.** Choose an area to develop and practice. Whether you learn from a book, workshop, mentor or online course, home in on areas to further your communication skills. Maybe it's Toastmasters or an improv class; maybe it's mastering non-verbal communication, brevity or presentation skills. Find ways to build your confidence speaking up and out. No time for that? Then grab your phone and record yourself during your next online meeting or ask for consent from the other meeting participants to record the video call. What can you learn from your participation? There are many ways to take your skills to the next level.

- **Reflect back; plan forward.** Look back and think about how you ruled meetings over time. When did you feel at your best? When did you feel defeated and thus retreated? What stories helped shift your behaviors and how in turn did others perceive your presence and impact? What is working that you will keep doing, what will you stop doing and what will you start doing?

Which reframe was most useful for you in this chapter on standing out in meetings?

From _____ to _____ .

5

OWN IT, FLAUNT IT, GET IT

From "My results should speak for themselves" to **"I speak for myself, my results and my goals"**

FAITH WAS FINALLY up for partner at the company where she had spent most of her career. She worked tirelessly; she moved to a new city to get known in a bigger market and she built valuable relationships both internally and externally with customers. Faith took all the requisite training programs and diligently applied the learnings to catapult her personal growth. She had unique expertise and built a business and a team with strong followers. She already made her firm a lot of money. By all accounts, she should be a shoo-in for partner. As the grueling panel presentation day neared, she asked if I would help her prepare for her pitch.

Faith walked me through her slide deck outlining her business case, and I was simultaneously struck by opposing impressions. On the one hand, her track record of results was incredible. I tried to poke holes in her data and pepper her with questions. Clearly, I didn't understand her business and technical skills to the level she did or the partner panel would. She responded so matter-of-factly to my questions that I began to feel silly. Soon she just waved her hand dismissively and said, "I have examples for that, I have stories for that; don't worry, it's solid."

On the other hand, I kept pushing Faith because, well, I guess I didn't believe her. She spoke sheepishly about her results and plan. Her tone of voice could only be described as meek and half-hearted. If her track record was so solid, I couldn't understand why she didn't come across as more confident, proud, enthusiastic. I didn't believe her because she didn't come across as believing in herself.

The situation compounded because she frequently used *we*, referring to her team instead of taking ownership for her results. I asked Faith who was up for partner: her or her team. I asked her what stood in the way of her speaking in the first person. What made her reluctant to use *I*? I asked her if she really wanted partner. What a silly question... of course she did.

Like most women, Faith didn't want to come across as bragging. She didn't want to appear arrogant. And most importantly, she valued her team immensely and didn't want them to think she wasn't giving them credit where credit was due. Faith believed that her results should speak for themselves. But do they? Is that enough? Are *you* willing to take that risk?

Faith was certain she had a great track record. She knew her business plan was solid. She was definitive in her desire to become partner. Now she needed to say it aloud and in such a way that the partner panel believed it as much as she did. She needed to speak for her results. She needed to own it, flaunt it and go for it. Let's take a further look at the false beliefs that are well engrained in most women and that initially held Faith back from speaking up:

- results are self-evident
- self-promotion is bragging
- managers should divine aspirations

"My results speak for themselves"

Think about it: results are voiceless, mute, unable to speak. The amazing report you just wrote can't speak. Paper can't speak. The big sale you just landed can't talk. The innovative idea you had can't tell a soul. Results can't speak; only people can. It seems a ridiculous thing to point out, like I'm engaging in wordplay and semantics, but it's actually a very important concept to internalize. You must highlight your results. If you don't tell people about the great things you've done and why they should bet on you for that next project, next meeting or next promotion, how will they ever know?

Faith realized that she was the only one who could share in her formal presentation why adding her to the partner ranks would be a great bet for the firm. And if she didn't, she was leaving too much unsaid and up to chance. There were only so many partner spots up for grabs, fewer than the number of people in the running. Faith had to get comfortable fast with tooting her own horn. If she downplayed her accomplishments, it would work against her. Everyone else would surely champion themselves in their pitch presentation. It left too much up to chance to let her story be inferred. Unfortunately, many women don't make this same decision.

A 2019 study published in the *British Medical Journal* found that there can be much at risk when women downplay their accomplishments while speaking and in their writing. The study revealed a distinct difference in the language that male and female researchers used in describing their published works. The team analyzed approximately 6.2 million general life science articles published between 2002 and 2017. Clinical articles involving a male first or last author were more likely to present research findings positively in titles and abstracts compared with articles in which both the first and last author were women.

If you're wondering about why this whole first and last author thing is a big deal, it's because in this community, the first author is the main person who contributed most, and the last author is either the most senior or the person whose grant paid for the work. So first and last are the bigwigs. When the bigwigs were male, there was a big difference in how the work was written, and the difference was more pronounced in journals considered to be prominent or more prestigious.

The researchers focused on twenty-five terms that past research identified as distinctly positive. Men were more inclined to use these words in their titles and abstracts: *unprecedented*, *novel* or *remarkable*. If you think this comes down to simple word choice, you couldn't be more wrong. Titles and abstracts are what people use to determine if they should explore the article further. The researchers concluded that a positive presentation of research findings was associated with higher downstream citations (the number of times the work was cited by others). In the academic world, citations are a component of promotion and hiring decisions, and women were at a distinct disadvantage. Language matters. How we speak and write about our work matters.

What secret successes and superpowers are you hiding? Do the people who matter—those who can help you—know about your track record, your strengths, your development goals and your aspirations? What fantastic opportunities might you be missing out on?

"It sounds like I'm bragging"

A common reaction women have to talking about themselves is fear of sounding arrogant, conceited or boastful. *Talking about what makes you great is bragging. Asking for something is self-serving and that's not right. It's gross.* I hear this all too often.

A team did a rather fun survey called the Self-Promotion Gap to explore women's fear regarding self-promotion. They found that 77 percent of women surveyed could name something else they would rather be doing than talking about themselves in a room of strangers. Things like doing errands in the rain, cleaning the bathroom or giving up social media for a week. Really! Wow, we need to reframe this and fast. Just saying, give me the choice right now and I'd rather tell you my book is unprecedented, novel and remarkable than clean my toilet.

Why is it so hard for women to talk about themselves and their accomplishments? If you identify with this, you are not alone. In fact, you keep good company. I kid you not, as I wrote this chapter about being comfortable with sharing accomplishments, an example materialized.

I like noise when I write. Sometimes it's the TV, sometimes it's the radio. I'm not paying it attention; I just need something other than silence. It provides background noise that keeps me focused. And this time, even a nugget of a story. A clapping noise on the TV broke my concentration. I looked up from my computer. *The Rachael*

Ray Show had just come back from commercial break. I saw Rachael hold up her new book, which was published that week. It was different from her other cookbooks: this one was deeply personal, a hybrid autobiography and cookbook. It was time for her to do a thirty-second promo spot. I stopped and paid attention because Rachael was at a loss for words. If you know anything at all about Rachael Ray, you wouldn't describe her as ever being at a loss for words. But this is how I experienced her in those thirty seconds. A few words fumbled out of her mouth in fragmented and unconnected sentences. She then took a visible deep breath and said something like, "I just hate talking about myself... Listen, buy the book... If you don't like the stories, you can at least cook the food." She laughed nervously, rolled her eyes, put the book down and uttered a huge sigh of relief while she wiped her brow. She finished with "Whew! Glad to get that over with."

I was gutted for her in part because I knew exactly how that felt. I'm sure you do too. It's a completely normal response. Maybe she didn't get a pep talk in advance of this segment. She has every reason to be proud and yet she too hates talking about herself. It was such a wasted opportunity though. She had a captive audience of supporters. It's difficult to share information about our successes and accomplishments and yet we must. Rachael wants to sell books; you want to do interesting work. We all have to sell ourselves sometimes, despite the discomfort.

During her social psychology postdoc at Yale, Corinne A. Moss-Racusin found that both men and women felt discomfort when engaging in self-promotion activities. The main difference, however, was that men persisted despite the discomfort. Moss-Racusin's study, published in *Psychology of Women Quarterly*, found that both men and women feared that people wouldn't like them when they self-promoted, but women were more likely to let that stop them. She also said that women don't inherently lack the skills to self-promote, but it's a stereotype violation for them. The interesting thing is that while women have the fear of reprisal, few actually experienced it. Moss-Racusin concluded that women have internalized a cultural norm, a story where self-promotion is something women shouldn't do.

How penalizing is that cultural norm?

Marie-Hélène Budworth and Sara L. Mann also studied the area of self-promotion and modesty and confirmed that women face a double bind. Women faced social backlash when they behaved in ways that were perceived as immodest (*she's so out for herself*), and they were penalized professionally when they behaved in ways that weren't self-promoting (*I didn't know she wanted that promotion*).

Yes, I hate to say it, but it comes down to you're damned if you do and you're damned if you don't. Fair? Nope. Frustrated? Well, don't be. It makes the choice easy. If you're penalized no matter what you do, then you might as well choose the course of action that could potentially have a positive outcome. You can sit back and do nothing, say nothing and let things stay the same way forever. Let someone else change the double bind. Or you can fight the discomfort, take a risk, speak up and help change the world for the better one conversation at a time, for you and for all of us.

"My manager should know"

Have you ever said something to yourself like, *We were in the same meeting; you saw my contribution firsthand* or *I bust my butt to implement this project on time amid all the roadblocks; what do you mean that's worth a "meets expectations" performance rating?* Or how about *What do you mean you didn't know I wanted to be considered for that project or that promotion?*

We say these things to ourselves because we believe our manager should know. They should pay attention; they should see what we see; they should make the same conclusions. Our results and our actions should speak for themselves. That's a lot of shoulds.

The phrase "results speak for themselves" is an idiom that means "no further explanation is required." It would be nice if it worked that way. Unfortunately, it doesn't. We can't leave things up to human interpretation because we humans interpret things differently.

I know you already know this but humor me as I remind you of a basic tenet of human communication. You think you are communicating clearly, but others hear something completely different than your meaning because they listen through their own filters, experiences and biases. Same thing goes when someone is observing you. They watch to confirm what they want to see or expect to see. Or more than likely, they just aren't paying you that much attention to begin with. (How dare they!) Therefore, your belief that no further explanation is required doesn't hold water.

Even though your boss is in the same meetings as you, they aren't necessarily watching you; if they are, they may come away with a different conclusion than you do. They may not know how much effort went into building a relationship with that stakeholder who greased the wheels for them to get on board with your plan. Your boss may have breezed in for the final meeting and saw that the result was achieved, unaware of all the hard work you did in the background to get the positive outcome.

Many conversations are required in order for you to get a raise, a promotion or onto a key project. It is up to you to provide information to clarify and share understanding, intentions and goals.

Bianca worked in the media division of a large telecommunications company; her team was responsible for negotiating contracts and rights for productions. Her boss was stressed with a new challenge: working with a composer for an original score. Bianca enthusiastically offered to help and was shocked when her boss gave her a dubious and somewhat cynical look. Bianca did self-advocate, thankfully, and reminded her boss that before joining this organization she ran her own production company where she produced twenty-five films and worked with many composers. It was all right there in her résumé, clear as the light of day. Her boss had interviewed her, for goodness' sake. The facts spoke for themselves. But as it happens, her boss forgot. She hadn't read her team's résumés in years and the topic of a composer had not come up until then.

"You can't be that kid standing at the top of the waterslide, over-thinking it. You have to go down the chute."

TINA FEY

It's frustrating because we expect our managers to remember all our glorious skills and accomplishments from last year and last week. But they likely don't, and we can either get angry about it or we can share information and tell them again. And again and again. Many studies have shown that it takes between six and twenty repetitions for us to remember something. So go ahead, be a broken record.

When you believe your results speak for themselves—in Bianca's case, the accomplishments on her résumé—it puts too much onus on others to remember details about you. Sure, there are great people leaders who remember all the skills, accomplishments and dreams of their team members. But sadly, they are rare; most managers are struggling to get through their days too. They run from meeting to meeting with cranky bosses, coworkers and customers. My intention is not to let crappy people managers off the hook, but you need to make it easy for others to help you. Unless you work with people who have eidetic memories (photographic memories), you need to help them out.

Alma fell into this trap. She expected her manager to not only remember her career aspirations but to be a mind reader too. Alma shared her painful story in a workshop I ran. Luckily, she can laugh about it now.

Earlier in her career, Alma was passed over for a promotion. She complained to her husband about the man who ultimately got the job and, in her estimation, was much less qualified than her. She was livid at her boss. Her husband asked Alma if she'd let her boss know she wanted to be considered for the job. "No!" she said. "He should have known." You may roll your eyes at this example, but I have heard this kind of story many times. Many times.

Alma was clear on her career aspirations, but she didn't share them fully with her boss. She thought that her stellar track record would be rewarded and that her hints at progression were enough. She expected that her results would speak for themselves and she would be asked to apply for the new role.

A great people leader would have proactively discussed the opportunity with Alma. A great people leader would sponsor women and encourage them outright to apply for career advancements. But my years of leadership development experience confirm that great people leaders are a rarity.

Make it easier for everyone, yourself included, and let people know how awesome you are and what other awesome things you want to be doing moving forward.

Activity: Your self-advocacy story

Let's examine your mindset toward self-advocacy. You know how sometimes someone says, "Go ahead, there's no right answer"? Well, sorry, but this isn't one of those times. As you go through this activity, you will recognize how you *should* answer. That's okay if you're not there yet: be brutally honest with yourself and see how far away you are from the self-advocacy ideal. Once you know your starting point, you can plan to make movement in the right direction.

What words or phrases immediately come to mind when you read the phrases below? Jot down the themes that pop into your head.

Self-promotion _____

_____

Gaining visibility _____

_____

Speaking up _____

_____

Building profile _____

_____

Which statements—the left column or the right column—are closer to what you say to yourself?

"I shouldn't have to ask. My work should speak for itself."	"Others don't always know. My job is to let them know."
"I don't have time for this; I have real work to do."	"I get to shape my future. Others need to know how to help."
"It doesn't seem like the right time to ask for something."	"It's never a great time for the company to risk losing great talent."
"This is all about me, me, me."	"Others can advocate for me too."
"I'm bothering people with unimportant personal stuff."	"I'm helping by informing them of ways I can have greater impact."
"I'm being arrogant."	"I'm proud of the value I add to the organization. I owe it to myself. I deserve it."
"I'm bragging."	"I'm sharing information. I'm making my work visible."
"This is hard and uncomfortable."	"Talking about myself is hard, but that's how I grow and make change for the better."

What helpful mindsets do you hold, and which may be holding you back? What new stories can you tell yourself?

_____

_____

_____

Reframes

You deserve all the opportunities you can muster! It's time to start sharing vital information so that others can help you. You must speak up for yourself, so your boss does not miss or misinterpret your career aspirations. You must create connections to influencers and decision-makers, and draw visibility to your strengths inside and outside the organization, so that you can continue to do the things you love or try something new that stretches you. You must embrace this way of thinking about the critical skill set of self-advocacy.

From lost in the crowd to "up front and center"

Faith, from the opening story, didn't speak in the first person when she was going for partner because she was afraid of throwing her team under the bus. She didn't want to be seen as self-serving or to deprive her team of the recognition they deserved. There are many times when we need to speak using *we*—when we're working in collaboration and when we want to share success with others. But often we have only one shot to get that job, that promotion, that stretch assignment.

In case you're wondering, Faith did make partner. (I had left you with a cliff-hanger, I know!) She shifted how she spoke during that partner pitch and, more importantly, how she felt. There was congruence between what and how she was talking about herself, her results and her plan. She was believable and it paid off big time.

If the I/me issue is something you struggle with, like Faith did, you need to start telling yourself a different story. You know the old saying, "There is no *I* in team"? Well, that saying was created to address the annoying people who cannot play nice with others. You know who they are. I argue that there certainly is an *M* and an *E* in team. Claim it, think it and say it. You don't have to wipe the words *team* or *we* out of your vocabulary completely. You can still use the words as you describe your accomplishments. But be sure that you make it clear what you did and what you led. What does that sound like? Here's an example of something you probably have said to your boss at one point or another:

> The team worked really hard to bring this to the finish line. I'm very proud of them.

And you leave it there. You feel good. Your team was awesome. You gave them credit. That's what a great leader does, and doesn't that magnanimity make you look good too?

All of those things are true. But it's left open to interpretation. What did *you* do specifically? What value did you add? The listener doesn't know and is free to make it up if they choose. Did the team flounder their way through the project, leaving a wake of stress and shaky relationships across the organization? Did they execute flawlessly without you, rendering you obsolete in your manager's eyes? Or, worse, did they succeed despite you micromanaging and getting in their way?

What you can say instead:

> The team worked hard to bring this to the finish line. I made the strategy and their roles clear, then got out of their way. Some coaching was needed when they encountered stakeholder resistance, but they learned how to navigate better. I'm proud of how much they grew individually and as a team in the process. My decision to stretch the team really paid off. They are humming along, which allows me to focus on the strategic priorities of... *(Thank you, chapter 3.)*

Saying it this way still shows the valuable contribution of your team. It also highlights what you did as a leader beyond profiling the team to your boss. You articulated strategy, you coached, you invested in their development and you probably fought some fires in the process. Your strengths are highlighted and you've left a positive impression of your skills in your boss's mind. It shares vital information about your leadership capability. Think of three of your competencies (skills, knowledge or abilities) and have your *I* statements ready to go, up front and center.

You don't have to be a people leader for this to work. If you're an individual contributor, you can still share what you did and what the rest of the team did. Take the opportunity to let yourself shine alongside the team. It's not an either/or conundrum, it's a yes/and. There's room for both *we* and *I*. Share your role too. It doesn't negate theirs. It adds to it.

From walk the walk to "talk your walk"

As girls, we were raised to be modest. Bragging and boasting were unbecoming. You, like most of us, were probably taught to focus on *we* first, not *I*. It's not surprising that sharing your accomplishments and your skills feels like bragging to you. It feels self-centered or fake. And being self-centered or fake, we were taught, is wrong. Emotions attached to bragging are guilt, shame or embarrassment. And those emotions prevent you from sharing valuable information with others who are assessing your performance to potentially provide you with growth opportunities or to sponsor you for a new job.

But what if you could leverage a different emotion instead? What if you could draw on a genuine positive emotion you feel when you do something great? What about pride? Pride is an internal feeling, an emotion related to self-worth, and it's critical to feeling confident in your success.

You don't go to work to toil away tirelessly to produce horrible results. You want to be successful, do great work and be rewarded for the value you add. It feels good when you have success. It feels great when you know you have a skill that is a strength you can lean on. Leverage those emotions when you share your information with others.

By definition, to brag is to speak with exaggeration and excessive pride. I don't advocate anyone do that. The key to your delivery is balance, or what I refer to as confident authenticity. You might even try using those words: "I'm *proud* of the track record of results I have *accomplished* and am *confident* that I will add the same value in this opportunity." Or how about:

> Great news! Not sure if you heard yet but we fixed the bug. I wanted to share with you the feedback that Josh gave on my performance through the process. [And then you insert all the amazing things you did using *I* statements, maybe peppered with a *we* statement, but not too many or you'll ruin the recognition recipe.] I'd like to take part in similar cross-functional teams again. I heard you're putting together a team for the new product. Am I being considered? I sure would like to be and am confident I can add similar value.

How does that sound? Great? Then get going. Gross? Well, start small and keep practicing.

Keep in mind that voicing your accomplishments and strengths is one part. You must also ensure that your non-verbal cues support how proud you feel and the confidence that engenders. An incongruence in your words and actions can lead to the perception that you are not confident in your abilities.

A colleague asked me to meet with Tasia, who was recently downsized and looking for new employment. Although I was in no position to offer her a job, I said yes because networking is important (more on this in chapter 6).

Tasia is a talented individual with great experience. As we were speaking, I noticed an interesting pattern. Every time I asked Tasia a question about her accomplishments or strengths, she looked down at the table and averted eye contact. I was genuinely interested in her abilities so that I could potentially refer her for opportunities I learned of through my network.

I debated whether to give her this feedback, then reminded myself that I had her best interests at heart. At the end of our conversation, I told her how much I enjoyed chatting with her. I then asked her permission to provide an observation I made during our discussion that may be helpful as she enters the many formal job interviews to come. After I described the pattern, she was both surprised and gracious. I let her know that her résumé and track record were stellar, and she was undermining them with her non-verbal cues. I didn't want that for her, because she was accomplished and deserved success. Tasia went on her way and I didn't know what she did with that feedback.

On International Women's Day a few years later, I received this message from her:

> To celebrate this year, I am sending out messages to a few of the women that have inspired me with rewarding career advice. I remember when I met you for coffee at your office a few years ago when I was in transition. You shared some feedback about my change in expression when I talked about my personal accomplishments and eye contact. It wasn't the type of feedback that I expected to receive going into our meeting and it was so valuable. Thank you! I think back to our conversation often and have shared it with others as an example and passed it on to others that would benefit. Sometimes it's the small things in life that can have a big impact, and that's what your coaching tip did for me. Thank you again!

So go ahead—own your accomplishments, flaunt them and look 'em in the eye while you're doing it.

From hidden talents to "showcase my value"

Many women have told me that they don't want to bother their managers with conversations all about "me, me, me." They don't want to be a nuisance or a bother. It feels self-centered and selfish. If you feel that way, try thinking about it like this: you are providing vital information that helps your manager make important people and project decisions. You are informing your organization's leadership that you are interested in contributing further, that you are committed to the future or that you are interested in helping fill the pipeline of future leaders. You are not a nuisance; you are sharing ways you can be of more value to the team or organization.

Sadie works for a large organization. She's been there for twenty years; it's all she's ever known. Sadie has moved around departments and roles, which has given her a robust network and a well-rounded skill set. But now she's bored. She gets bored often; not because she's lazy, but because she learns so quickly.

Sadie has been named a high-potential leader, won multiple excellence awards and exceeded expectations on her performance reviews often. But currently she's working for a lackluster manager and stuck at the senior manager level. Her goal is to become a director and soon.

When you're in a large and ever-changing organization like hers, it's about getting known and known for the things that will help you advance. Sadie constructed a plan and set off to network with a variety of VPs to share her skills and aspirations. She reluctantly called it her "promotional tour" in an effort to muster up courage for the conversations with senior leaders. When I asked her how it was going, she said it was going well, but she couldn't shake the feeling that this whole promotional tour was "all about her."

Through our conversation, Sadie realized that she's her happiest when she's helping to solve a big problem, when she can take a mess and bring process to it. That's why she gets bored quickly. She comes into a situation, learns about it, assesses what needs to be done, galvanizes a team around the required changes and then puts a plan in action—with incredible results. After a year or two, when things are running smoothly, she's ready to tackle the next challenge. Sadie is most engaged when she's adding value to the organization in ways that many people can't. It's a desirable skill set.

That's how she learned to reframe the promotional tour in her head. She benefits by continual stretch and growth *and* the organization benefits tremendously too. She reframed from hiding herself and her talents to showcasing her value. Sadie entered her meetings with an eye to looking for new and vexing problems she could help solve for the organization. In that scenario, they all win. She needn't feel guilty anymore about meeting with VPs and explaining what she's done, what she's accomplished and how she's ready to add value somewhere else.

If by this point, you're still not sure about *self-promotion* or *selling yourself*, how about you stop using those words. Most women abhor those words too. I get it; they feel self-serving and smarmy and ick.

Self-advocacy is a better term but not one that rolls off the tip of our tongue on a daily basis. At its core, self-advocacy—what I've been talking about in this chapter—is about speaking up for yourself, your needs and your wants. I particularly like a definition I found on a parenting site aimed at building this critical skill in students.

> Self-advocacy is learning how to speak up for yourself, making your own decisions about your own life, learning how to get information so that you can understand things that are of interest to you, finding out who will support you in your journey, knowing your rights and responsibilities, problem solving, listening and learning, reaching out to others when you need help and friendship and learning about self-determination.

Wow, hey? We want children to learn these skills, and yet somehow we forget as grown women that we must use these same skills too. This all comes down to believing in your value, knowing what you want and engaging with others to get it. In short: own it, flaunt it, get it.

1:1:1 Plan

Once a week

- **Catch it.** Identify when you minimize your accomplishments or skills. Do you chalk up a success you had to luck, timing, the team or something else? Catch yourself. Don't do it. Take ownership for the part you played in your own success. Voice it; share it. Talk about your strengths with confidence. Look up and smile with pride while doing it. Remember not to minimize compliments either; say thank you to those who recognize your success.

- **Beam positive.** Notice when you talk solely about the negative aspects of a project. Admit it: when someone asks you how it's going at work, more often than not you bring up what's not working, who is being a pain or why things aren't going as planned on the project. Reframe to speak about a success first: something positive you did, how you're taking ownership of something, what insights you've gained. Demonstrate your skills in change, leadership, collaboration and overcoming obstacles. Save the moaning (which, yeah, sometimes we need to do) for one trusted person.

- **Advocate for all.** Bring visibility to other women's successes, skills or accomplishments. We're in this together. Make a pledge with trusted colleagues to give public and private kudos about one another to important stakeholders. This might not happen every week but train your brain to watch for opportunities to celebrate others.

Once a month

- **Talk the walk.** Reflect on which important stakeholders (managers, sponsors, mentors, senior leaders or others, internally and externally) know your track record, your potential and your career aspirations. Choose one person who can benefit from having more visibility to your achievements and aspirations. Ask them to have a networking or career conversation. As you ask for advice from them, find ways to tell them about how you're looking to add value next. Share your strengths and accomplishments with genuine pride. Stick to talking about facts and data and it will feel like sharing vital information.

- **Track your truths.** Keep track of your accomplishments and successes. Use whatever method works best for you. Create an email folder for feedback from others. Journal or keep a hard copy file folder. Keep an ongoing draft of your résumé, LinkedIn profile and/or bio at the ready so you can quickly insert a win or success metric. Compile your notes and read them often. It will bolster your confidence. It will also make conversations flow as you won't have to grasp for details and examples.

- **Raise others up.** If you are a people or project manager, consider implementing a shout-out during your monthly staff meetings. Recognize an individual or team during each meeting. The intent is to create a culture that celebrates achievements and lets others understand important skills and wins of people who may have less profile. When fairly and genuinely instituted, it becomes a self-perpetuating cycle. If you are a team member, suggest it to your manager.

Once a year

- **Pen a bio.** Write a short bio for yourself that captures your strengths, achievements and accomplishments. Be bold; highlight your superpowers! Pretend you need a blurb for a book jacket, an introduction for a huge conference you will speak at or a Nobel Prize. Yes, really. Don't say you're a teacher; say you are an educator and an inspirer of future generations. Don't say you are a great admin; say you are a master diplomat and negotiator and an organizational wizard. This will be tough, and you need to shoot for the stars. It's hard to write these things about ourselves.

That's the stretch. Draft a paragraph or two and then refine it with an eye to being as bold as you can be. Then share it with a few trusted advisors. Revel in your results; be proud; believe it; live it.

- **Manage your manager.** Performance reviews are an obvious time to share all your vital information. Really prepare for this conversation and share your strengths genuinely and proudly. Think about how you'd like to stretch and be prepared to make your asks. Arm your manager with information to provide you profile and exposure with their boss and other senior leaders too. If your employer doesn't have a formal process, or it's far into the future, then ask your manager for a career development conversation.

- **Extend your reach.** Reflect on where you have profile in your organization, sector or community. Where do you need to build more profile, and where can people learn about the value you have to add? Begin to advocate for your results and your aspirations in new places.

Which reframe was most useful for you in this chapter on self-advocacy?

From _____ to _____ .

Hang on a minute!

I'm a big believer in practicing what I preach. I've struggled with every tactic in this book, and so when I suggest something, know that I've tried it too. The first draft of this book contained my personal horror and triumph stories at every turn. My editor said it came across as a memoir. Apparently, I'm not famous enough (yet . . . as per chapter 1) to write a memoir. She didn't exactly say that, to be fair, but that's what I took away.

So, here we are at the end of chapter 5 and I've just professed to you the importance of self-advocacy. I would be a hypocrite if I didn't ask at this point for your support, wouldn't I?

My personal vision is to help as many women as I can to feel empowered, inspired and to live their best life. My aspiration is to assist as many women as possible to lighten the mental load and be fearless at work. You'll read more on my manifesto in the conclusion. But for now, I'm going to own it, flaunt it and go for it. So here it is . . .

I'm proud of this book. I'm overjoyed with the impact I've had on the women in my leadership programs and I'm confident I can have further impact. I'm honored to highlight the stories of so many women I have met and whose lives we've mutually transformed.

If you're enjoying this book, if it's helping you think differently or if it gives you some ideas to implement, will you please help spread the word? The more people who have access to the book, the more we can help change our collective stories.

Take a minute now or wait until the "pull on your heartstrings" ending to write a review for me on your favorite online retailer's website.

Thank you for your support and let me know how I may be helpful to you (that's some chapter 6 foreshadowing).

6
THINK *WHO* BEFORE *DO*

From
"Results and productivity are king"
to **"I'm the queen of connection"**

I T WAS THE third time this group of women were coming together for a high-potential leadership program at one of North America's largest banks. Celia, one of the participants, yelled out from the back table, "Wait, before we start, I have a story to tell about the meeting after the meeting."

At the previous workshop a few months earlier, I had mentioned an article that talked about networking, informal decision-making and organizational politics. Specifically, I had referenced the topic of pre-meetings and post-meetings. Usually inclusive of men, meetings before and after the main meetings are where alliances form and decisions are made. Celia had been particularly vocal during this discussion, scoffing at the notion.

"There are no secret meetings! There's only one meeting," she had said. "It's in my calendar and I go to it with the others." Celia had a good network. She didn't want to believe that she was being left out of something.

"I don't know if it's true for you or not," I had said to the group, "but start watching for it and see if it exists."

Now I was interested to hear Celia's story about these meetings. "Go ahead, the floor is all yours!" I said. In her animated style, Celia recounted what happened once she started paying attention to see if a separate meeting dynamic did indeed exist. She went to her regularly scheduled management meeting and when it ended, she did what she always did: jumped up and rushed to the door so she could get to her next meeting on time. She noticed that the other women in the room had already vacated. And then it hit her. All the women are gone, and the men are still hanging back in the room. The conversation about the article flashed through her mind. *Screw it*, she said to herself. *I'll be late to my next meeting. I have to find out what this is about.*

Celia said it was one of her most uncomfortable moments as she backtracked into the meeting room. She literally walked backward slowly, hoping to appear inconspicuous. (Not sure she succeeded, just saying.) She sauntered over to the coffee urn where her male colleagues were standing. She poured herself a cup of cold coffee and joined the group. As she listened, she was flabbergasted. They were still talking about the meeting topics. They were reopening decision points and challenging them. She had the distinct feeling that what had been decided in the on-the-books meeting might not be the final decision after all.

I waited for what Celia would say next. I expected her to be angry, to feel jaded or to decry exclusion. But she didn't. She was curious. Celia said she went to her boss that day and told him about the article and what she observed. "Explain this to me: what is this dynamic?" she asked. "And more importantly, how do I get in on it?"

Unlike most women, Celia didn't throw up her hands in disgust. She didn't profess to take the high road, knowing full well she might miss out on some critical information and relationships. She accepted that informal networks existed. She had been certain that her strong formal network would have carried her along, but she realized that she was missing a key part of the dynamic often referred to as organizational politics, the process of using an informal network to gain power and accomplish tasks to meet a person's wants or needs.

Celia didn't assume that she was excluded; she sought to understand more. She didn't believe her male colleagues were deliberately sabotaging decisions or intentionally creating a secret club. Her response was to dial up her networking further and build relationships with key influencers. She knew that she had to extend her circle of influence and become more politically savvy. Today Celia is in an executive role and oversees a North America–wide mandate.

Unfortunately, research would suggest that Celia's mindset toward networking and organizational savvy is not the norm. Her story illustrates the importance of having a strong, diverse network *and* knowing how to leverage it. But for most women, the word *networking* recalls painful chitchats with strangers, schmoozing and sticky name badges that either never stay put or leave that annoying residue on your favorite top.

Even worse, when I say *organizational politics*, the immediate reaction I get from women is that it's smarmy, sucking up and a complete waste of time. It conjures up notions of backstabbing, favoritism and secret clubs. Some even call it evil.

Most people understand what networking is. It's an activity or a process to connect with people and share information that may benefit one or both parties now or in the future. We know we should do it, but it often gets pushed to the wayside, even though research has repeatedly shown that people with broad networks are more successful. Investing time in building networks is important, and the astuteness to navigate and leverage connected networks is critical too. Let's look at the reasons why women are more reluctant to build and leverage the relationships required for their success:

- prioritizing real work over fake work
- keeping groups of people in discrete buckets
- confusing savvy with slimy

"I have real work to do"

I spoke on a panel of senior executive women and one of the questions posed to me was "Tammy, I get that networking is important, but how do you make time for it?" I responded with "Coffee and lunch are your job. Building relationships is the work of leadership. You schedule it in your calendar like everything else."

The mistake many make is believing that real work is equated to tangible results. Complete the quarterly report; build the software code; address the patient concern; teach the class; make the product—if I can see it, it's real work.

If you equate real work with tangible results, then imagine all the fake work you engage in. Endless emails, minor meetings and pointless parties. If I'm honest, a lot of these activities often do feel wasteful. But that is why highly effective people—those who prioritize their time and energy to accomplish their personal and professional goals—know how to triage emails, get the most from meetings or say no to going in the first place and use social events to build culture and relationships.

There is a tremendous amount of work you do or should be doing that doesn't immediately yield results, seems invisible or takes you away from tangible tasks. Take developing others, for instance. Coaching, mentoring and providing feedback to build talent are critical. Or how about figuring out who influences a decision on your project: who the key decision-maker is who will ultimately approve it and how best to communicate with them so they'll say yes. This is also a critical activity but can seem labor intensive when you'd rather be sitting at your desk perfecting the slide deck (a tangible task) you'll take to the big meeting.

If you want to be more effective in your current role or grow into a new one, you must stop distinguishing between real and fake work.

Sitting around chatting with others feels like an indulgent use of time, a break or a distraction from the real work. It may be if that's how you use that time. But what I'm referring to is deliberately connecting with others to do better work, become more knowledgeable and advance your career.

The reality is that none of us can do our jobs on our own. We are interconnected and fundamentally dependent on many people inside and outside the organization. And yet most of us see relationships as nice to have but not necessary.

Most women prioritize *doing* the work over understanding *who* the people are that influence the work, approve the work or say what work you'll be doing now and down the road.

Celia made this realization when she stopped herself cold in the doorframe after that meeting. She realized that she and her female colleagues were rushing off to do the next thing on the list. Celia recognized in that moment that she needed to understand who was staying back, who influenced decisions and who would ultimately make the final call. Thinking *who* before *do* helped Celia unlock a critical flaw in her story. It's not enough to know who is in your network; you must also leverage those relationships to understand the people dynamics, which influence the work.

Ask yourself, Do I squirrel away and only involve others when absolutely necessary? Do I network when I have time (i.e., never)? Do I rarely attend social events or keep a low profile if I do? The problem with this approach is that you create no influence, little profile for you or your team and are often overlooked as serious potential for different, bigger or better things.

"I don't want my worlds to collide"

"My worlds are colliding!" was the famous phrase uttered by George from *Seinfeld*, mortified when his romantic world and his friend world collided. For women, it's the fear of uniting work and home networks; the unwritten rule is often "I have a home network and a work network, and never the two shall meet." Herminia Ibarra, a professor of organizational behavior at London Business School, called this "separate spheres," finding that women had less overlap in their networks than men did.

I fell into this trap many years ago while on maternity leave. I met a great group of women in my neighborhood. We exercised together, drank wine together, laughed together and essentially kept each other sane. We got to know each other like sisters, or so we thought. Soon after I returned to work, I facilitated a senior leadership program with an important customer. I finished setting up the room and began to welcome the leaders as they came through the door. To my surprise, in walked Ellen, from my mom group.

"Get out! You work here?" I asked. My inside voice said, *And you're a senior leader here. How did I not know that?* "No way, you're my teacher?" She laughed.

None of us in the mom group really knew what each other did outside of being moms. We didn't want our worlds to collide. But it doesn't work like that. While it's embarrassing to admit, it taught me a valuable lesson about interconnection.

Monica Stallings of the Wharton School studied network preferences between men and women and who they preferred to seek career advice from. In this study, Stallings confirmed earlier research that men's networks have a higher number of what is called multiplex ties. These are relationships that provide multiple resources including friendship and professional resources. She found that men tend to seek friendship from those men who also provide access to organizational resources.

I saw how women keep separate spheres firsthand during one of the networking courses I taught. The workshop participants worked on a specific networking goal and then wrote down who in their existing network could help with that goal. I asked for a volunteer to share their thinking. Ella spoke up first because she desperately wanted help from the group on her scenario. She was deeply conflicted.

Ella was a scientist by background, looking to make a career change to a global health sciences company. At this point, she wanted more information in a specific area to see if her longing to work at this company was justified.

Right, let's start with the obvious. I asked her if anyone in her current network worked at the company or knew people who did.

"*Well*, my sister-in-law works in human resources there," she said nervously.

"Woo-hoo—awesome!" I returned. *She's hit the gold mine*, I thought, having learned my lesson about uniting work and home networks (bright gold star for me).

"I can't go talk to my sister-in-law about work!"

"Are you on bad terms?"

"No! She's lovely; we get along great."

"Okay, so . . ."

"I can't just go up to her at a family gathering and start talking about work."

"Uh-huh..."

By now the others in the workshop were seeing the ridiculousness of this situation and began to throw out advice masquerading as questions.

"Could you ask her to have a separate conversation at another time?"

"Would you feel more comfortable having an evening phone call with her?"

"Right, so just tell her you feel awkward but would be so totally grateful."

Ella was befuddled and paralyzed. She could not fathom asking her sister-in-law for insight into the organization she worked for. Even though she wasn't asking for a job (she was in the research phase), it still seemed weird to her.

This is what women do either on a grand scale or small scale. Thankfully we helped Ella reframe her thinking from *This is weird; I could never ask that* to *I have access to an insider whom I'm super close to and will tell me 100 percent honest information because she has my best interests at heart. How lucky am I?*

Maintaining separate home and work networks takes more effort. It also limits your access to important information and people. Maybe it's time to let your worlds collide.

"I feel inauthentic and gross"

Women, more so than men, feel inauthentic when building and leveraging relationships with members in their network. Ibarra attributes this to a number of factors, including that people prefer to interact with those most like them. She notes that the "likes attract" principle is well established in social sciences: in general, we are most comfortable with people like ourselves. Women are often outnumbered and outranked in organizations, so creating connections with those unlike us feels onerous and manipulative. Ibarra states that the more we differ from key stakeholders, the more likely that we'll see an intentional approach as disingenuous and calculating—all about selfish gain, using people and engaging in unmeritocratic ways of advancing one's career.

This reluctancy to leverage relationships for one's gain was studied recently through interviews with high-profile female leaders working in large German corporations. The researchers found that women felt morally conflicted about leveraging their network and had hesitations about over-benefiting from social connections.

Over-benefiting? What does over-benefiting even look like in a career sense? You get offered too many opportunities, too many ways to have deep and meaningful impact, too many benefits, too much money? What? That's crazy. So why do we feel that way?

One reason is that women underestimate their value to the network. Women hesitate leveraging networks for fear that they cannot return the same value; it feels morally wrong to engage in an ask in the first place. If I can't return the favor, then I don't want to make the ask. If I get something and do not reciprocate, then I am over-benefiting from the relationship.

But networking is a long game and reciprocity doesn't have to happen overnight, which is why we maintain connections over the long term. A former colleague, mentor and wise networker once counseled me to end every networking conversation by asking the other person, "And how can I be helpful to you?" When you ask this question, don't second-guess your value. You have information and insight that is unique. You do! I promise you do.

I remember asking for a quick coffee with an executive who was visiting my office from out of town so I could connect, gain profile and stay visible. This wasn't a comfortable thing for me to do, but I did it regardless at my manager's suggestion; I knew it was good for me, like the cod liver oil my mom spooned in my mouth before school each morning. I learned about the exec's priorities and his challenges. I told him what I was working on and the impact it was having. I thanked him for his time and ended with "Is there anything I can do to be helpful to you?"

He stopped and stared at me for what felt like an eternity. He then smiled and said, "Thank you for asking that. You've taken me

"Networking is a lot like nutrition and fitness: we know what to do, the hard part is making it a top priority."

HERMINIA IBARRA

by surprise. No one has asked that in a long time." He then proceeded to ask my advice about how to enable and sustain change in our geographic location. I had a lot of insight to share, despite my initial feeling that someone two levels above me would already know what I knew. Our coffee went over the allotted time because I was providing value to him. That in turn upped my value in his estimation.

Another reason building and leveraging networks may feel inauthentic is because girls are socialized in groups to look out for the good of the whole. Engaging in activities that profit self at the expense of others feels dishonest, deceitful and disingenuous. This is why the notion of organizational politics is repulsive to most women as adults. The use of networks, informal decision-making and power feels one-sided and fake. But does being authentic really have to come at odds with this? Ask yourself:

- Is understanding who is in my corner inauthentic?
- Is knowing how the world around me works deceptive?
- Is being open about my goals, aspirations and agenda dishonest?
- Is talking to senior people about their viewpoints and feedback phony?
- Is putting myself in the shoes of decision-makers to understand their perspective backhanded?
- Is finding the informal routes to how decisions are made devious?
- Is prioritizing relationship building on a daily basis crooked? Is it, really?

This is what building good relationships and knowing how to use them is all about. It's not inauthentic; it's smart, it's strategic. If you said yes to any of these questions, keep reading for how to reframe the story you tell yourself about the importance of thinking *who* over *do*.

Activity: Your network story

You likely know networking is good for you, like a kale smoothie, but it doesn't often make it to the top of the priority or preference pile. Let's find out why and make it move up. Navigating and leveraging relationships at work (organizational politics) also needs to become a priority. Yeah, I know, but it does. Understanding the stories you tell yourself about your interest, your ability and the importance of these activities will go a long way. So before reading further, chew on these questions.

What stories are you telling yourself about the importance of networking and engaging in organizational politics? What helps you, and what holds you back?

_____

_____

_____

What stories are you telling yourself about your ability to engage in networking and organizational politics? What helps you, and what holds you back?

_____

_____

_____

What one big shift would you like to make?

_____

_____

_____

Reframes

Success today requires a stronger focus on relationships than it did in the past, because work is no longer as discrete and people are no longer as visible. Let's look further at how you can reframe your stories to create the relationships you need to become more influential, get more done with less stress and have abundant opportunities to do more of what you love. Sounds pretty good, doesn't it?

From preoccupied with performance to "prioritize people"

Carla Harris, vice chairman at Morgan Stanley, in her book *Strategize to Win: The New Way to Start Out, Step Up, or Start Over in Your Career*, argues that most people are focused on performance currency instead of relationship currency. We earn performance currency when we do great work and get recognized for it.

You strive for accolades and great performance ratings from your manager, don't you? Of course you do; we all do. And you need to focus on performance because it's the baseline to keeping your job and getting paid. But focusing solely on performance (i.e., the real work, the tangible results, the doing) often leads to more work, and more of the same work. It's not enough to get noticed for new or different things like key projects, promotions or pay raises.

Relationship currency, however, is what helps you advance further, Harris argues. Without sponsors, those who actively advocate for you, you will have a harder time seizing opportunities. It's critical to build relationships across, up and outside the organization.

I knew two successful executives who understood this well. One was sociable, a natural networker, a born connector you might say. The other was quiet and struggled to connect deeply with others. But both understood their success wasn't just about the results they achieved; it was also about the information they obtained, the trends they needed to be on top of and the alliances they couldn't live without.

If you needed to know something or someone, they knew how to connect you—either directly or a few phone calls away. Yes, a real, actual phone call. These connectors actually talk to people live. They will hang up and try again if they get your voicemail. You needed talent, they knew someone. You needed a new service provider, they had recommendations. You needed the pulse on the place, they had it. One made it a habit to reach out to his counterpart at the direct competition and similar organizations for every role he was in. They wouldn't share confidential information, of course, but they shared themes, insights and experiences. Who knows better what challenges you're facing than someone doing the same job in the same industry? The other set monthly lunches with colleagues so he could keep on top of the myriad of challenges that occur when working across the organization. You might say one was an extrovert and one was an introvert; it didn't matter. In their own ways, they prioritized *who* over *do*, and because of this they were able to achieve extraordinary results. The use of their strong network yielded insights others didn't have and a strong group of supporters for what they were trying to achieve.

The good news is that women are natural networkers and wired for connection and relationship building. Yes, even the introverts. Thankfully, networking comes in many forms. It can be done one-on-one or in groups, face-to-face or online.

No one has endless time to network, but everyone needs relationships in three key areas. Herminia Ibarra and Mark Lee Hunter outline three forms of networking that are required to be successful: operational, personal and strategic. I have built on their definitions below.

- **Operational network connections:** These are the people you need to know to get your work done both effectively and efficiently. They tend to be internal connections but may be external depending on your role. You know who these people are because you couldn't do your job without them. These are colleagues in your department and in other departments you interact with. It can also be suppliers, customers or partners. Are your relationships with these people strong or strained? Are you making each other's lives easier or harder? Your focus here is initiating, deepening or repairing these critical connections.

- **Personal network connections:** These connections are all about development, growth and advancement. They can be internal or external individuals who provide you with information and further contacts. Managers, mentors, sponsors, coaches, trusted allies and loving critics are examples. They are the people who give you profile, the straight goods and have your best interests at heart. Personal network connections can be strong ties or acquaintances you meet at events or on LinkedIn. In order to gain benefit from these connections, you have to maintain a certain level of contact, make asks of the contacts and offer to help in return. Most women do not have these connections in abundance or at all; if they do have them, they are reticent to ask for their help.

- **Strategic network connections:** These are the people who help you keep on top of the impact of broad strategic issues within your organization and industry. They can be internal or external connections. They serve a future focus and that's why connecting with them feels frivolous or an activity to be put off for more pressing matters. But imagine how being more informed about your areas of expertise, competitive landscape, market trends or research can give you a leg up in conversations with important decision-makers. You find out this information from professional associations and conferences, external experts, colleagues in different areas of your organization or senior leaders who have access to different information and insights than you do. This network is critical if you want to be perceived as strategic, experienced and connected.

I find most women are strong in the first type of network, dreadful in the second and mixed in the third. Where are you strongest? Which area needs work?

As you master the skill sets at your level, you need to focus on relationship currency by building a strong network of advocates. This is probably the biggest gap in your network. It is for most women. You need to start building this group of supporters, sponsors and senior allies now. Building relationships is not optional. It is not something you do when you have time. In fact, having a coffee chat with others may make the difference between your success and your failure. Go book one now. You can't afford not to.

From separated and small to "connect and capitalize"

Joan, a seasoned executive and board member of a global professional services firm, addressed the female partner hopefuls at a development workshop I led. The main focus for this module was building a strong network, and when I asked the organizer which senior role model could speak to the importance of networking, Joan was the obvious choice. It was her superpower: network woman, leaping levels by uncovering insights, saving people by offering information in a pinch and uniting the world in person and online one conversation at a time. Joan's "super connection" was not a result of being extroverted or attending the most events; she was curious and saw the world as interconnected.

Joan shared many practical tips with the women at the workshop and warned the group not to discount anyone as a possibility for their network. This was the secret to interconnection. We see many people every day and assume they are not like us. We assume conversations with them will be fruitless, she said. Then Joan started talking about toilets and plumbers and we became utterly confused.

Joan's basement toilet had broken, and she needed it fixed urgently. Her family was big into hockey and for years they boarded players from all over the world. The hockey boarder was arriving soon, and the toilet needed to be fixed ASAP.

When the plumber arrived, Joan told him why it was so important it was fixed properly and urgently. Because she shared her reason, they got to chatting more. Joan found out that the plumber's brother also boarded hockey players on occasion. Since the hockey boarder community is quite small, Joan thought she might know the plumber's brother.

"What's his name?" she asked. When she heard the answer, her eyes bulged. The brother was none other than the chair of a board she was dying to serve on. Joan, being the consummate connector, asked for an introduction to the plumber's brother. He gave it, she called him and voila, she subsequently got a board seat. If Joan kept her home network and her work network separate like most women do, she never would have made this connection. If she hadn't struck up small talk with an unlikely source, it would have taken her much longer to get a seat on that board, if at all, she said.

Networking was easy for Joan because she was curious and saw the world as interconnected. She took a minute to strike up a conversation and see what connections were shared. Then she made no qualms about asking for connections or information. And she was just as generous about giving hers.

After that day, I decided to start trying it. I started chitchatting with people everywhere: in the elevator, at the grocery store and in line-ups. At one point, my daughter asked me, "Mom, why are you suddenly talking to strangers all the time? Aren't we not supposed to talk to strangers?" "Well, it depends," I said.

Research has shown women's networks are often smaller, closer knit and leveraged primarily for social and support reasons. Men tend to have larger networks with more acquaintances that reach into many worlds. More connections mean more access to people and information. Is one approach better than the other? The reality is you need both.

You need the close contacts to survive and to thrive. But if you want to be more effective or if you're looking to advance, you need to expand your influence through a broader collection of individuals. Odds are you will find these contacts in interconnected worlds, like Ella did with her sister-in-law and Joan did with her plumber. I know there is safety in similarity and comfort in likeness. But the world really is your oyster when you start connecting to it.

The same holds true for inside your organization. See what connections exist with colleagues across your organization. Stop doing your work in a separate silo and start looking at who is out there to share insights and be on your side.

From avoided like the plague to "pursue influence"

Leveraging network relationships and navigating the organization are often seen by women as inauthentic. I'm here to tell you it's not smarmy, slimy or self-serving; it makes you quite strategic and savvy. Well, okay, it can be smarmy and that's when we say people are being *political*. But you're not going to do it that way, are you?

Organizational politics has become a catchall term for the bad behavior of a small number of self-serving individuals. A few self-absorbed jerks have given organizational politics a bad name. When Jim coerces Bob into siding with his course of action by withholding resources or threatening repercussions, then that's bullying or blackmail, and it needs to be addressed as such. When Julie reopens and reverses a decision in a back-room meeting, then lack of transparency and poor decision-making processes need to be called out.

Thankfully multiple researchers, management experts and authors are helping to reshape how we define and think about organizational politics. The authors of *Political Skill at Work*, Gerald Ferris, Pamela Perrewé, B. Parker Ellen III, Charn McAllister and Darren Treadway, have researched organizational politics for over two decades. They remind us that being politically savvy does not equate to being manipulative. When it's properly applied, it makes good things happen, both for those who use it and for the organizations in which they work.

Those who are positively political have four things in common:

- social astuteness, meaning they can read and adapt to different situations

- interpersonal influence, which inspires others to act and adopt their ideas

- networking ability to build the relationships needed for success

- sincerity in making their intentions known and acting in the interests of others

These four elements of positively political people are all about paying attention to the *who*. With this framework, why do women continue to be appalled by organizational politics and how can we overcome it?

In *The Influence Effect*, authors Kathryn Heath, Jill Flynn, Mary Davis Holt and Diana Faison share the insights from their survey of senior executives on differences between men and women when it comes to office politics. They found that women were more than four times as likely to say men were better at politics, while men were nearly twice as likely to agree men were better. Further they found that both women and men disliked engaging in politics, but it's a skill that is associated with rising to higher levels.

In an interview, Heath shared that women can become better at politics if they redefine it in more favorable terms. The key is not to see political skills as a manipulative, inauthentic or a competitive activity, but as gaining influence through managing relationships. If you care about something, you need to be able to influence effectively. And you can build and leverage relationships to get support for your ideas, projects and career. At its core, being politically savvy in your organization means you know what's really valued, what's important and how to get it done, who has the most influence to help you and which battles are worth fighting.

But wait, there's more.

Being politically savvy can even lead to less stress! Wait, what, less stress? Yes, less stress. Pamela Perrewé, Gerald Ferris, Dwight Frink and William Anthony published a white paper in *The Academy of Management Executive* arguing that leaders who have political skills—social astuteness and the ability to engender confidence, trust and sincerity—are better able to cope with the chronic workplace stressors they encounter. They suggest that interpersonal control allows you to interpret situations in less aversive ways. What does that really mean? It means you can communicate with someone sincerely and confidently by letting them know you know what's going on and it displeases you; when it's out in the open, you can work it out like mature adults. And that helps you sleep better at night. Thankfully it's a skill that can be learned. Whew!

Rewrite your story now about organizational politics. Don't wait as long as Sharon did to rewrite it for herself.

Sharon is an executive at a professional services company. She's worked in the industry for decades, including at many of the firms in her sector. She knows her customers, what the end users need and the evolving trends. After a few years at her latest company, she wanted to launch a product that she viewed as critical to her customer base. It would automate processes and provide online content and tools for customers. It wasn't revolutionary; it was table stakes, and her company was way behind. Customers were looking for lower cost options and competitors were squeezing profit margins. Without this product, her company would be viewed as leagues behind the others and risk losing customers.

For Sharon, this investment was a no-brainer. But like any technology implementation, it cost a lot of time and money. Neither her colleagues nor her boss shared her urgency and the project stalled. Sharon knew she needed to change course when she started to feel what she could only describe as needy. She realized her mindset was counterproductive and it was impacting her success.

Sharon felt guilty as she went from meeting to meeting trying to garner support. She feared that people were seeing this project as a personal win for her. Was she selfishly taking away investment resources needed in other areas? She was hesitant and felt like she was asking for favors. She questioned herself, *Am I being political?* Gasp! Sharon had spent her entire career pooh-poohing all things political and avoiding getting caught in the crosshairs of heated battles. Yet here she was doing the same and it didn't feel good; it felt smarmy. She felt self-serving and powerless. And she knew that it translated to a lack of success with her stakeholders.

Sharon wasn't ready to let go of this project. She reframed her story by reminding herself that this product was good for their business. Her customers were asking for it and the end users would benefit immensely. She needed to win this battle for them! That perspective always drove Sharon's success. It's what has kept her customers loyal to her and what has kept her passion alive in a dramatically evolving space. Sharon knew she had to change her mindset and change the conversations she was having. She went in with new resolve to show the benefits of her business case. She created urgency by showing what was at risk for their business. She fought for their customers.

In the end, Sharon got influencers on board and was thrilled when the president finally voiced how critical this investment was. Sharon told me she felt powerful, and it felt good. Sharon is in her mid-fifties and was surprised that it had taken her this long to realize that organizational politics could be used for good. She was surprised by how good it felt to feel powerful—a power based on achieving what her customers needed, not a power based on self-ishness. Her multiple one-on-one meetings, her targeting of key influencers and her passionate and forceful defense of customer market share wasn't dirty, it was authentic. Sharon regretted how long it took her to reframe from avoiding politics like the plague to pursuing influence. It had undermined how she operated and made the process take a lot longer. She was focused on *doing* instead of on *who* she was doing it for and *who* she was influencing.

If after all of that you still don't like the term *political*, why don't you just go ahead and eradicate it. Stop using it; stop thinking about it. Be smart, savvy and strategic. Get good stuff done; make choices and excel in your career. That's what building and leveraging relationships and understanding how to navigate them can do for you. It feels good when your ideas get accepted. It feels great when you are recognized for your accomplishments and successes. Why wouldn't you use a process that helps you get more of that? Start thinking *who*, not just *do*.

1:1:1 Plan

Once a week

- **Don't go it alone.** Notice moments when you feel like you haven't seen anything but your desk, computer screen or wherever you do your work for a while. Notice when you feel lonely, disconnected or like a robot. Pay attention to when you feel like you don't have enough information or insight. You may be focusing too much on performance currency rather than relationship currency. Find time to connect with others or build important relationships.

- **Monitor eye rolls.** Watch for moments where you feel yourself pooh-poohing political skills in action. Do you roll your eyes at Ben when he mentions he had lunch with an executive and highlighted the project you both worked on? *Damn you, Ben!* Do you chalk it up to shameful schmoozing? Or do you see what you can learn from his approach? *Touché, Ben, touché.* Pay attention to moments where you can reframe from smarmy to strategic.

- **Listen deep.** At a meeting you're attending, choose to put on a different listening lens. Don't just show up and pay attention to what you normally would. See what you can learn about what drives individuals. Choose someone and ask yourself, *What can I learn about what's important to them, what pressures they face, what worries them, what makes them have a certain viewpoint?* Practice understanding what motivates people. Test your theories either one-on-one or in the meeting as appropriate. For example, you might say, "It seems you aren't on board with this plan because it doesn't yet address the impact on employees. Equity and fairness appear critical for you. Is that a fair statement? Tell me more." Listen for *who* before *do*.

Once a month

- **Seek tips and tactics.** Connect with someone you believe to be a great networker or savvy navigator. Ask how they approach building and leveraging networks. Ask them the best way to influence up in the organization. Ask who the key influencers are in the organization from their perspective. Probe for how they handle political situations. Ask how they've handled circumstances with competing priorities and stakeholders at odds with one another.

- **Make a map.** Identify the important stakeholders in your project or role and connect with them. Determine if they are champions, supporters or resisters and why. Keep the map up-to-date and capture insights you're learning along the way about how to navigate people, decisions and opportunities. Make another map for your career goals, aspirations and personal vision.

- **Connect as habit.** Consider sitting next to someone new in a meeting, chatting with someone you don't know or picking up the phone instead of emailing, texting or messaging on Slack (yes, really). Send a networking contact a message that you're thinking of them. Maybe it's spending a few minutes on increasing your professional online presence. Get into the habit of intentionally connecting with people to extend or strengthen your network or to learn more about how the organization and decision-makers work.

Once a year

- **Plan the (net)work.** Determine which types of network connections you need to strengthen. To get started, choose one operational, one personal and one strategic connection to build. If you do more than that, good for you. But at minimum, set this goal. Prioritize purposeful network meetings. Schedule them as you would any other meeting. If people cancel, rebook. Again and again. Don't take it personally. Review and update your plan at the end of the year.

- **Work the plan.** Reflect on what has changed in your organization— the culture, the important stakeholders, the processes. How do you need to rebuild relationships in the new reality? Who do you need to meet with? Who can help you be successful? Who has left, who has stayed and what does that mean for how things get done? What is shifting in importance? Update your network plan as a result.

- **Up your value.** Make yourself more valuable to your organization and your network by gaining insights on your area of work. What event do you need to be at to learn or get known? What experts do you want to hear from or read about? Where might you want to do a presentation? Plan this intent with respect to your network goals. Don't just go or do it because you feel you have to or should; determine how it will meet your goals and personal vision.

Which reframe was most useful for you in this chapter on building and leveraging a network?

From _____ to _____ .

7

LIGHTEN UP, BRAIN

From
"I'm barely
hanging on"
to **"Let go"**

YOU'RE HARRIED, STUCK in traffic or delayed by a long-running Zoom meeting. Your stomach is growling because you skipped lunch again to finish up an urgent task. It's the witching hour—kids fighting, dog barking. You're angry at your colleagues because they won't stop talking. You're angry because dinner will be late again. Your guilt sets in. *Why didn't I take out the frozen chili last night that I made for hectic moments like this?*

Your mind starts spinning out of control. You recall the perfect meals from your childhood. You hear the voice of an acquaintance who said, "Oh no, we have a hot meal on the table every night." You tune back into the meeting and realize you missed an important comment; go figure. You feel increased dread as the seconds tick on.

We've all been there many times. The guilt, shame, embarrassment, anger, resentment—take your pick, you've felt it. I sure have. Then I remind myself of a fellow working parent who told me to cut myself some slack and stop making things so hard. She shared a tip that could save not only a single night's dinner but years of meal guilt. What is this magic she speaks of? Muffin tin dinner. Huh?

Reach for those muffin tins and open the fridge and cupboard. Fill each hole in the pan with vegetables, fruit, protein or dairy. Crackers or pita; dips or sauces. Leftovers, hot or cold. Anything goes. Save a hole at the top for a drink. A small glass, sippy cup or juice box fits in perfectly. The last hole is for a yummy treat that must be eaten last. That's the only rule.

Spread out a blanket and have an indoor picnic or place the tray on your kids' laps for a midweek movie night or a pretend flight to an exciting destination of their choosing. Watch as they zigzag through the holes in the tin or follow an orderly path. There's a personality test hidden in there somewhere, I'm sure. They will love it. My daughter is a teen and still asks for muffin tin dinner.

My colleague's tip wasn't just about making a quick dinner. It was about cutting myself some slack, seeing there was another way, lightening my mental load.

Studies have repeatedly shown that women suffer higher levels of anxiety than men. According to experts, these differences can be explained partly by hormones, partly by brain chemistry and partly by the upbringing that has conditioned women to feel more responsible for the happiness of others, such as a spouse or children. Striving to be perfect, succumbing to constant guilt, ruminating and doubting all take their toll. It creates toxic inner monologues, unrealistic expectations and the dread of never keeping up.

Muffin tin dinner is but one way to tell yourself a different story, to reset expectations, to give yourself a break. Muffin tin dinner is a metaphor for all the small acts that help us rewrite our stories. Tonight you're not failing; you're exceeding your kids' expectations by doing something fun. (And healthy and easy and fast, but they don't need to know that. They just know you're awesome.)

The burnout and emotional exhaustion that women experience are about more than dinnertime struggles and will not be fixed with a single muffin tin dinner. Obviously. What this story highlights is one important component: self-compassion. It has been shown to have the biggest impact on our happiness, resilience and our ability to deal with stress. This chapter is a starting point to identify the stories you tell yourself where you criticize and judge instead of having compassion for yourself.

This chapter sums up the ways women make their heads and hearts heavier. These are the false perceptions, strivings and talk tracks that weigh us down at home and at work. These are the ways you need to tell your brain to lighten up! Let's have a look at which false perceptions resonate with you:

- constant quest for perfection
- persistent feelings of guilt
- relentless rumination

"It has to be perfect"

The illusion of perfection plagues most women. It's the quest to be the perfect partner, mother or daughter. To have the perfect career, the perfect home, the perfect look. We think that to have it all, we should be perfect in everything we do. As girls, we are rewarded for good behavior, for looking nice and for getting along. And the magazines, TV shows and social media we consume don't do one bit to end the madness.

This is compounded by a society that has created an unwinnable pull between being the ideal worker and the ideal mother. The ideal worker is a concept that was generated in the 1950s and included men who worked full-time with devotion, available at any time to do whatever was required to get the job done, no matter the cost. The ideal mother stereotype is, well, you know, perfect. Patient, nurturing, devoted, community minded, a great chef, baker and seamstress. Whatever the situation calls for, really. The pull between these two ideals creates expectations that are unachievable for any functioning human.

Do you feel that no matter how much you give it's still not enough? Do you feel like you are failing as a mother, sister, friend, partner, employee, caregiver? It's a phenomenon that women face more than men both at home and at work.

Unfortunately, it has created overzealous pride in women for a job well done as they seek to conquer each task with seeming ease to the outsider. The result of this vicious cycle is that it compels you to strive for perfection in all things. It's caused women to grip tight and control everything within their grasp. It's the plague of the perfectionist's vise grip. And you know what I'm going to say... it causes more harm than good.

Alice Boyes, clinical psychologist turned writer, offers sage advice to those who strive for perfection. She says that most people think of productivity as how fast they can get everything done. I bet you do. It's a common myth. Productivity isn't about getting more done: it's about making intentional choices about what you get done. Perfectionists rarely see this important distinction.

The quest for perfection causes three big problems. First, you think everything is important and fail to distinguish between unimportant and important. All tasks are deemed worthy of your time and energy. This thinking also reinforces taking control and micromanagement.

Second, striving for perfection can trigger a duty to overperform, overprepare or overdeliver. This causes you to spend more time on tasks than is normal or expected. Do you worry that others won't like you, respect you or reward you if you fail to deliver or don't exceed expectations?

Third, striving for perfection inhibits flexibility, which is critical for mental health.

Boyes says perfectionists fall into three general categories:

- those who take on more than they can handle, causing undue stress and potentially letting down those who count on them—which ironically is exactly what they're trying to avoid. *Yes, I'll take that on; yes, I'll do that too; sure, I have time to whip that up; no problem, I can; I can do it all.*

- those who avoid starting a habit unless they are certain they can achieve the goal every day, which leads to procrastination or missing out on activities that can be helpful or fun. *If I can't exercise for an hour and get in a warmup, workout and post-stretch, then I'm not going to do anything because it won't get me the results I want.*

- those who engage in only the habits they can accomplish no matter what, risking compulsive behavior. *I invested two years in this; I will not give up until I become the best regardless of what it costs me.*

Does any of this resonate with you? Are you able to give yourself a break? Can you try something new or implement habits in a variety of ways? How is perfection holding you back or unnecessarily stressing you out?

"I feel *so* guilty"

Guilt is another form of self-sabotage. Both men and women feel guilt; however, numerous studies have found that women in particular are prone to feelings of guilt across all age groups.

Guilt is defined as an emotion we feel because we're convinced we've done harm. Guilt comes from many triggers: something you did (*I ate the entire cake myself*); something you didn't do but wanted to (*I forgot the school fundraiser again*); something you think you did (*Did my comments make him angry?*); something you didn't do as much as you could have (*I should donate more to that charity; they send me so many blasted beautiful return address labels I will die before I use them all up—I know, because I've done the math based on my average yearly mailing consumption*); or something you receive instead of someone else (*Janet has been here much longer than I have; she deserves the promotion*).

Feelings of guilt are everywhere. *My house is a disaster. I haven't called my mother in weeks. I'm not doing enough for the planet. Should I eat more vegan meals? I didn't make it to the gym again. Am I progressing in my career enough? My kids are getting too much screen time. I'm not taking enough time for myself. I am taking time for myself and it feels selfish. I still haven't responded to my team's email.*

And if you are a working parent, at home you feel guilty for not doing work. And when you're at work, you feel guilty for not being at home. It's a relentless, inescapable cycle of guilt.

Guilt and the realization that your family doesn't need you every second is a lesson Magdalena Yesil learned the hard way. Yesil was the first outside investor and board member of Salesforce and is highlighted in Julian Guthrie's book *Alpha Girls: The Women Upstarts Who Took On Silicon Valley's Male Culture and Made the Deals of a Lifetime.* Yesil was integral to helping rescue the company during the dot-com bust, but when Salesforce went public, she wasn't there.

Yesil made a decision that she still regrets today. Her son was sick, so she stayed home instead of standing next to Salesforce founder Marc Benioff at the New York Stock Exchange for the celebratory ringing of the bell. Upon reflection, Yesil realized someone else could have stayed home and her son would have been fine. It was one day of a mild illness out of hundreds that her child would experience. It was the only day that this momentous event would happen in her lifetime. She let guilt get the better of her and missed a career highlight. She is certain no man would have made that same call.

This line of thinking is so well engrained in society that it's not just women who have children that worry, it's also women who don't yet have children. A young woman reached out to me for career advice on LinkedIn because she saw we both went to the London School of Economics for our graduate studies. This young woman had not one but two master's degrees. She was brilliant and ambitious. She was deciding between two job offers: one at a top four consulting firm and one at a bank. Her family and friends were pushing her toward the consulting firm because, for all intents and purposes, it was what she was groomed for. She was struggling with the decision because the job at the bank seemed remarkably interesting to her and she assumed it would afford her more flexibility to have a family.

She looked young to me and I asked if family planning was on the near horizon for her. She laughed and said, "I don't even have a boyfriend!" And yet she was making her first foundational career leap based on which opportunity would provide her with a more family-friendly culture. The guilt, the responsibility, the pressure is pushing out great talent before they even enter. It needs to stop. Organizations need to step up in a big way to counteract this horrible undue pressure on working women.

Since the dawn of time, girls have been socialized to take care of the physical and emotional needs of others. Feed others first; tend to others first. Don't hurt anyone's feelings and keep the peace. Today women still endure most of the responsibility for keeping households running efficiently, not only with cooking, cleaning, laundry and shopping but organizing schedules, remembering holidays and special events for relatives and friends and planning parties (which must be done perfectly with gorgeous Pinterest-worthy picture proof).

This dynamic has been given a name: the human giver syndrome. The term, originally defined by Kate Manne, an associate professor at the Sage School of Philosophy at Cornell University, describes how women are more conditioned to believe they have a moral obligation to fulfill the needs of others at the expense of their own needs. The resulting guilt and anxiety leads to physical and emotional exhaustion. Are you a human giver who has given so much there is nothing left in the tank for yourself? Are you ready to tell yourself a different story—a story where you get to receive too?

"I can't stop thinking about it"

Do you constantly question yourself, think negative thoughts or refuse to let things go? Do you replay the same conversation over and over in your head until you can't sleep? It's called rumination and it's a serious problem.

Rumination is the process of thinking about a past or future event over and over again and attaching a negative emotion to it. It's unproductive because it rarely leads to useful action. It can lead to false assumptions as you rewind a conversation or scenario, each time seeking to dissect more layers of emotion and innuendo until you've created an entire scenario of assumptions, context and motivations that may or may not be true about the people involved. It keeps you in a downward spiral of inaction, entrenching grudges, fears or despair. It's unproductive and potentially dangerous.

Sadly, it is well documented that women engage in rumination more than men. I could give you examples of rumination, but something tells me you know exactly what I mean. Well, okay, here are some of the ways the women in this book have ruminated.

Over and over again in her mind Sophie played the question of why she needed to work when her husband earned enough for the family, which implied that her ambition was a mark against her motherhood. Megan constantly questioned if she was good enough to be promoted to senior leadership. Marissa relentlessly reminded herself that her ambitions were selfish and could be put on the backburner. Olivia couldn't get it out of her head that she was a failure in her career because she'd decided to step back when her children were young. Melanie told herself daily she wasn't moving fast enough and that more hustle would get her promoted quicker. Jessica worried regularly that her current organization was the only place she could have success and that she could outlast the toxic team that kept her down. Anna couldn't stop telling herself she had to add value to everything, reminding herself of everything she didn't do as she lay awake in bed each night. Sara couldn't let go of the anger, replaying her conversation with Mark where she let him dump his work on her, calling herself *stupid, stupid, stupid*. Heidi couldn't let go of the fact that she was always the flip chart capturer, berating herself for not speaking up and making herself an equal. Carla told herself many a time that she was not strong enough to have impact with her fellow executives as she did with her own team, then regretting that higher-ups didn't know how good she really was. Laura began every meeting reviewing all the ways she was too junior, too young, too quiet to speak up. Irene boiled in the feedback that she had no sense of urgency for months. May blamed herself after every single meeting for remaining silent. Faith reminded herself constantly that saying *I* and *me* and taking owner-ship for her success meant throwing her team under the bus. Sharon couldn't let go of the story that she was being self-serving, replaying every conversation again and again looking for political trip-ups . . .

Enough!

We never let up on ourselves. We stew in self-deprecation, bathe in burdens, wade in worry, drown in distress. *Am I good enough, smart enough, driven enough, old enough, young enough, experienced enough, selfless enough, selfish enough, bold enough, modest enough?* Lighten up, brain.

What can't *you* let go of? What do you play over in your mind and attach a negative emotion to that holds you back? There is another way. Say it with me: yes, there is.

Activity: Your expectations story

You likely walk around with a lot of expectations in your head. Expectations for yourself and those around you, expectations for what can get done, when and to what standard, to name a few. That frame of mind means you will always feel weighted with too much to do, too much to take care of and too much to accomplish. This chapter is about reframing expectations. Before you continue, answer these questions to determine the ways you create a heavy mental weight.

What stories do you tell yourself about perfection, about guilt? What causes you to experience guilt? What negative thoughts, fears or angers ruminate in your mind? Capture a few honest statements.

_____

_____

_____

Read the statements you wrote and notice how they make you feel. Draw a picture that represents how it makes you feel—a sketch, symbol or emoji; no worries, nothing fancy is needed. That goes double for you perfectionists.

What would be possible if you could change these stories? What would it take to lighten your mental load? Draw a picture of what could be.

Reframes
....

Most of us succumb to unrealistic ideals at times. You are not alone in trying to get the perfect result. Everyone feels guilt. We all get in our heads and can't let things go. But we also know what it's costing us. We know what alternate possibilities exist. It's time to let go of the things that no longer serve you, that make life harder than it needs to be, that hold you back. It's time to lighten up, brain.

From gripping tight to "let up"
....

Corrine is a talented lawyer in a demanding career. As her career took off, her entrepreneurial husband, Raj, decided to leave the traditional banking world and begin his own consulting business. It gave the family increased flexibility and allowed time for the many community initiatives he loved to lead. Raj is energetic and enjoys being involved in all their kid's activities. He relishes learning new things like... cutting hair. "How hard could it be?" he said. Raj bought scissors and clippers and watched a few YouTube videos. And thus the family barber/stylist was born.

One Friday evening, Corrine commented to Raj that their son's hair was getting a bit shaggy. Raj agreed and said he'd get to cutting it that weekend. Saturday passed and their son's hair isn't cut. Sunday morning arrives and the hair still isn't cut. Sunday afternoon rolls around and no haircut. By this point, Corrine is beside herself. She and Raj talked about this on Friday and it's Sunday afternoon. The weekend is almost over!

Is your blood pressure starting to rise? Do you relate to this story? Maybe not the haircutting husband specifically but tasks that are allocated to people in your circle?

The mistake that many of us make is taking on items on other people's to-do lists in a quest to ensure everything is done (perfectly). Whose list has the haircut on it, Corrine's or Raj's? If you said both, then you've got some reframing to do, my friend. The task belongs to Raj, but Corrine has also put it on her own to-do list. She can't relax until the haircut is done. Would the world end if a nine-year-old went to school for another day with shaggy hair? No, of course, it wouldn't. It's not worth the stress. And that stress only got worse.

On Sunday afternoon, Corrine was tired of waiting for Raj to cut their son's hair so she got out the clippers and reiterated Raj's mantra, *How hard could it be?* After a few swipes of the clipper to her son's head, she realized that it did in fact require some practice. Desperately, she yelled for Raj to come and fast. Then the "What are you doing? I said I'd do it!" conversation ensued. Thankfully, they ended up having a good laugh about it later.

If you find yourself in a similar situation as Corrine, have a frank conversation or let it go. You have enough on your own plate; don't add to it. Lighten your mental load. Be honest: Are you carrying around tasks in your head that aren't even yours? Do you define perfection by getting everything done on time in the correct way? That definition is great for a lot of things, especially at work. But how many times could you instead say good is good enough? A haircut that can wait another week is an appropriate time to let up.

While we're talking about letting go, it's not solely about allowing others to own their own tasks; it's also about allowing them to own the way they're done. Psychologists refer to this phenomenon as maternal gatekeeping, when moms control dads' household responsibilities and/or interactions with their children. It's common and difficult to recognize and stop.

Here are examples of the ridiculous things I have heard women say: "I fold my kid's clothes because they don't do it right"; "I don't let my partner order pizza because they do it wrong"; "My kids hate when their dad packs their lunch. He really does make bad lunches."

If you relate to any of these statements, even a little bit, ask yourself what impact it may be having. Will your kids learn anything if they are not allowed to do it imperfectly? Does it matter in the grand scheme of life how the shirts are folded? Is ordering a pizza really rocket science, a skill that requires an advanced degree in computational cuisine logistics and distribution? Is it maybe time for the kids to take responsibility for making lunch themselves?

"Talk to yourself
like you would to
someone you love."

BRENÉ BROWN

You might think this is silly stuff. It's just one thing here or one thing there; what difference could it really make to let go? I challenge you to watch for one week all the things you "own" at work or at home and see how long the list is. How many things do you oversee, watch, remind or nag to get done … perfectly? I bet there is a long list of things clouding up your head. That accumulates to create heaviness.

Start small and learn to focus on the upside of letting up. I'm learning to live with a constant speckling of socks on the floor. When my husband and my daughter walk into the house, the socks come off almost before anything else. It's like the socks are made of lava and they just can't wait to rip them off. It gets so bad that sometimes multiple pairs of socks pile up on top of each other in multiple locations of my house. It used to drive me nuts. It still does some days. That's when I remind myself to just let it go. Let up. Own what I own. Nagging leads to bitterness; picking the socks up myself worked for a while before it led to resentment. I realized that letting go of the little things benefits my work, my health and my relationships. I know one day I will dearly miss seeing those socks on the floor. I know that day will come far too soon. That's how I help myself reframe letting up.

From paled with guilt to "glow with gratitude"

Claudette is a talented teacher who was offered the position of principal at her school. She didn't even need to apply; the administration sought her out for her natural leadership abilities. But she questioned whether she could handle the job and whether her family could handle the time commitment the more demanding role would mean for her. As we talked about the opportunity, I reminded her that she had the confidence of her board and superintendent. She was a natural. Sure, she didn't have as much administrative experience (yet), but she'd be supported along the way. It was a great opportunity for her to grow in her leadership and earn more money as she looked at the final phase of her teaching career before retirement.

But there was more at play. Claudette was a self-professed type A personality. A bit of a control freak. Having grown up on a farm, she valued home cooking, a clean house and helping out a neighbor. She always brought over muffins and other food to those who could use a helping hand. While Claudette enjoyed helping others, she felt guilty asking for help for herself. She felt guilty that her husband and kids would need to pitch in more if she took the promotion. She felt guilty that she may need to hire someone to help with cleaning and watching her kids before and after school. Guilt, guilt, guilt.

In the end, Claudette accepted the promotion. She accepted that her family was completely capable of stepping up. In fact, they were benefiting in the process too. Her husband enjoyed trying out new recipes on Sundays, his day dedicated to cooking and preparing meals for the week. He installed a small TV in the kitchen right smack between the barbecue and where the Instant Pot sits on the counter. Their son is learning to cook alongside Dad while they cheer on their favorite football team.

Claudette's kids followed a chore chart to pitch in and learn responsibility. Once they hit the requisite number of stickers (because she's a teacher, of course there's a beautiful poster on the wall with colorful stickers), they earned pocket money. They now pack their own lunches, regularly clean the house and are responsible for dinner one night a week. It's been a joy watching them advance from picky eaters and simple recipes to more complex palates and meal preparations.

I asked her if she had second thoughts about taking on the principal role. Not at all, she said. Her family is just fine. She is grateful that her family is supportive and grateful for the opportunities it affords for all of them. Once Claudette let go of the guilt stemming from the belief that everything was solely her responsibility, she could see that the promotion was possible, even desirable. When Claudette reframed her guilt to gratitude, she saw the upside of the very things she had felt guilty about in the first place.

Having gratitude is critical to our well-being. Robert Emmons, the world's leading scientific expert on gratitude, reveals why it is good for our bodies, our minds and our relationships. Those who are grateful—who practice being thankful and return that kindness and appreciation in turn—experience a magnification of positive emotions, increased ability to block toxic or negative emotions, more stress resistance and a higher sense of self-worth.

It doesn't mean, however, that by practicing gratitude regularly all the bad emotions simply cease to be. Claudette won't magically become a purple aura, devout, Zen yoga machine. (That's who I used to think practiced gratitude. Now I am proudly grateful and savor it up with the best of them.) But it does give her tools to tackle the times when guilt creeps back in. For gratitude to have the best impact, be sure to focus it on *who* you have and *how* things happened, versus *what* you have. Claudette is grateful for her family *who* stepped up and is benefiting in the process and for *how* the board sought her out to lead.

The guilt of the working mother is epidemic. In my work with female leaders, I hear story after story of fears about reentering the workforce after having children. *Will my kids turn out okay? Will they feel loved and cared for? Will I be perceived as a bad mother?* These are the confessions I hear. All this doubt and guilt swirling around in the heads of bright and ambitious women. If you're a working mom, you've probably had these thoughts too. There is reason for hope, however, for working mothers (or future mothers) and there are role models too.

Jane Fraser, the first female CEO of a major Wall Street bank, shared refreshing advice she received from a mentor with the audience of *Fortune*'s Most Powerful Women Summit in 2020. Our careers are measured in decades, not years, she said. We don't need to be in such a hurry and can take a step back if needed. Fraser recounted how grateful she was to carve out precious time with her kids during the period she was working part-time as a partner at McKinsey. She said it was instrumental to not only her family but to her professional achievements as well. She reminds mothers not to be in a rush to have everything all at once. Fraser is convinced that her success is owed to her time with her family. She is proof that pauses need not be forever and that if we have a goal and focus in mind, they can be achieved regardless of timing. (Remember chapter 2, and look up, look out to the horizon.)

There is more good news we can be grateful for. A Harvard study undertaken by Kathleen McGinn and her colleagues found that daughters of working mothers grew up to be more successful in the workplace than their peers. They earned more and were more likely to take on leadership roles. Sons of working moms were more likely to grow up making a more significant overall contribution to child-care and household chores. Furthermore, children under fourteen who were exposed to mothers who worked for at least a year grew up to hold more egalitarian gender views as adults.

Being a working mom can have positive impacts on children that outweigh the benefits of staying home. It's time to drop the guilt, no matter what choices you make. I know, it's easy to say and harder to do.

Start by trying to understand where the guilt is coming from. Is it because you feel responsible for someone or some outcome? Is it because you have wronged someone or because you didn't live up to an expectation set by yourself or others?

Determine which of your values and beliefs are driving the feeling of guilt. My guilt about hot, home-cooked meals seven days a week, for example, stemmed from my stay-at-home mom who cooked, canned, froze and stored everything from the garden. To this day, my mom still says, "Oh, tonight we're just having soup for supper." She says it with a dejected, guilt-ridden sigh. There is absolutely nothing wrong with a hot bowl of homemade soup for dinner (or a can of tomato soup for that matter, with soda crackers and shredded cheddar cheese, of course). It's actually amazing! There is no need to sheepishly apologize for that.

When you feel guilt, you need to determine where it's coming from. What is contributing to those feelings of guilt? Are the beliefs and values triggering the feelings of guilt valid? Is there anything that can be changed? If so, move to action. Call your mom; have that uncomfortable conversation with a friend; talk to your partner... whatever it is. If the guilt is unfounded, then tell yourself a different story, and most importantly treat yourself with compassion. My house is messy, but I'm grateful my family is healthy and happy. You missed that bake sale? Oh well, put the next one in your calendar. Pick up cupcakes or donuts. Be grateful you remembered. Haven't responded to your team's request yet? Tell them you're grateful for their work and their patience. Stop apologizing while you're at it too. Late to the meeting? Don't apologize; say thanks for your patience or nothing at all. No excuses, no guilt, no apologies—just gratitude.

From ruminate, ruminate, ruminate to "reflect, release, repeat"

I listened with rapt attention as a retired executive who was also an experienced board member addressed a group of female executive hopefuls. She was asked, "What is the single most important lesson you learned over your career as the lone female amid a sea of male partners?" She responded that she was much happier and more successful when she learned to "just get over herself." This meant not ruminating incessantly about every decision, blaming herself when she had a setback, taking everything so seriously or holding on to grudges. When she got over herself, she could project the confidence of a leader. Not only did this lead to greater success, but it also allowed her to sleep better at night.

One theory is that women ruminate more than men because they tend to focus more on interpersonal relationships. Caring about what people think about you, your capability or your ideas is ripe territory for rumination.

It's hard to get control of what someone once described to me as the "itty bitty shitty committee" that takes up office in our heads. These are the voices that make you question yourself, that tell you you're not good enough or that make you cling to unproductive feelings past their expiry date. Over time, rumination leads to cynicism, unhealthy relationships and burnout—none of which are helpful for productive functioning at work or home.

Rumination is when you rehash how you acted or what you said in a certain situation repeatedly. It keeps you stuck and anxious. How do we stop doing it though? Do we have to wait until we're retired to have the wisdom of that female executive? Gosh no! Learn the reflect, release, repeat formula now and benefit forever.

Reflection is deliberately thinking over an experience with the purpose of learning from it. There is a positive intent to learn and a goal to focus on what you can change or control. Positive reflection leads to positive action. When we reflect, we are also reminded that learning is a success in and of itself, even when it doesn't feel like it in the moment.

The next part is to release: let go of the things you can't change or control. This means not letting a past event define you or your future. Ruminating keeps you stuck; releasing moves you through the present and into the future.

Rumination can be hard to snap out of; otherwise we wouldn't do it so much, would we? It doesn't feel good, nor is it good for us. You know who also ruminates a lot? Cows. That's where the word comes from. Rumination is the action of a cow chewing cud. Picture it in your mind. Go on, get that picture clear in your mind. You've seen it: a docile Holstein standing in the sun amid the bright green grass. It's chewing slowly and lazily. Over and over and over. That's your brain when you won't let go. Lighten up, brain!

The next time you ruminate, create a distraction by thinking of that cow. Distraction is a key strategy in snapping out of ruminative states. If the cow doesn't work for you, use another distraction strategy. A friend learned a strategy from a therapist for when all else fails. Move your hand up and down saying, "Cancel, cancel, cancel." It really works for her and for me as well.

Perhaps you can choose an activity that you enjoy or that challenges your mind. Literally get your mind off the problem. Exercising or spending time in nature, for example, has been shown in numerous studies to reduce rumination and increase mental health over the long term. Mindfulness and meditation have been shown to free your mind, as you learn how to be aware of your thoughts and feelings and over the long term how to be less reactive to unwanted automatic thoughts.

If that's not for you either, then try changing the questions in your inner monologue. Counter negative thoughts by fact-checking. Ask, *Is my account of the events accurate? Will I never get an opportunity ever again? What is the possibility of me actually tripping in front of a room full of people? Will my child really get eaten by a bear if I let them go on the camping trip?* Challenge yourself to see that your thoughts may make little sense. Ask yourself what's the worst that can really happen. If your fear is totally unfounded, then let it go. If it's not, then ask yourself the likelihood of that worst-case scenario. If it's low, let it go. If it's high, then plan for it. Think of small next steps and write them down. Get your mind off *should have, could have, maybe will happen*, and plan to take action on what you can control.

Wharton organizational psychologist Adam Grant offers great advice for discernment when it comes to what we believe to be true. He says, "A sign of wisdom is not believing everything you think. A sign of emotional intelligence is not internalizing everything you feel. Thoughts and emotions are possibilities to entertain, not certainties to take for granted. Question them before you accept them."

What I love most about that quote is that it begins with wisdom. We often associate wisdom with old age. But wisdom is defined as having experience, knowledge and good judgment. No matter how old you are, I'm betting you have enough experience and knowledge when it comes to rumination to serve you a lifetime. Let's now lean on the good judgment aspect of the definition and not believe everything we think. We can be wise now. You can reflect on your learnings, release the negative and repeat.

Our brains are powerful and complex organs. That means you'll need to repeat the strategies outlined above. Get into a habit of replacing the expectations, guilt and perfection that swirl in your head incessantly. Instead of heaviness, fill your mind with positivity and lightness. At least once a day, for example, tell yourself what you're good at, what small steps you have taken, what success you've experienced, why you deserve happiness or what you're grateful for. You have enough going on in your life to worry about and get done. Don't increase the pressure by making it harder on yourself. Learn to love letting go.

1:1:1 Plan

Once a week

- **Detect and defeat.** Turn on your rumination radar. Pay attention to negative talk tracks that cycle in your head. Catch yourself in the act. Try the reframing strategies. Reflect, release, repeat.

- **Inhabit healthy.** Do something that sustains your well-being and lightens your head and heart. Exercise, meditation, sport, crosswords, reading, knitting, whatever. Focus your energy on something that does *you* good. Do it regularly—daily or weekly at minimum.

- **Rule out drama.** Lighten up your brain by refusing to engage in drama at work or at home. Don't get in the middle of arguments. Focus on the problem, not the people. Expending emotional energy can be more physically and psychologically taxing than physical or mental work. It's not worth it.

Once a month

- **Drop the guilt.** Notice when you start feeling guilty. Maybe you said yes or no to something and it's bugging you. Maybe you haven't yet done something. Maybe you haven't spent your time the way you hoped to. Whatever it is, identify when it is happening and keep track of it to identify patterns. Write down the big guilt trips and begin to reframe them.

- **Make a to-don't list.** Identify one thing you can let go of mentally. Start with a small thing and make it a habit. The intent is to remove the pressure of thinking you must do it all or own it all. Take it off your to-do list. Maybe it's a cleaning task or it's banishing your FOMO (fear of missing out) and not attending a meeting. Make a habit of lightening your load by letting something go.

- **Ditch perfect.** Choose something to do less perfectly. Let others help and don't criticize how they do it. Reset your expectations and become freer. Acknowledge up to three things that are important to excel at, then let your standards down for the other things. Embrace good enough.

Once a year

- **Expect relief.** Check in with your manager, partner, kids, parents or friends about the things you worry about. Are you really letting them down? Are the expectations you think they have of you aligned to the expectations you place on yourself? If not, reset expectations—yours or theirs. Make a plan to address it or let it go and tell yourself what a great job you're doing.

- **Secure support.** Having a support network is critical to mental well-being. Ensure you have a trusted individual or group to confide in. These are not people with whom you have to maintain a facade of control or perfection. These are the individuals that say, "Who cares if your house is messy, or you screwed up that meeting. You are amazing! Give yourself a break. Let's meet up and do something for an hour to take a load off." Surround yourself with those people. Life's too short to spend with energy suckers.

- **Check energy waste.** Reflect back and determine where you put your mental energy. What can you learn about when and where you worry, feel guilt or strive for perfection? What was a productive use of your mental energy and what was not? What wisdom can you bring forward?

Which reframe was most useful for you in this chapter on letting go?

From _____ to _____ .

CONCLUSION
OUR NEW STORIES

I WISH for a world where...

there are no separate programs for females or minorities

pay equity is no longer a topic and men aren't considered the default breadwinners

if you choose to work, you're not considered a bad mom

if you choose to raise a family full-time, you're not considered a cop-out

your commitment to senior roles isn't questioned if you have a family

men won't be threatened by your success

we don't automatically align *leader* with *man*

you can be assertive and commanding without being called names

you can talk about your accomplishments with pride and won't be judged harshly for it

you feel safe to be who you are

you don't fear being harmed or harassed

women hold one another up instead of tearing each other down

I believe this world is possible.

I HOPE that you...

believe in your potential

feel as though you can succeed at whatever you put your mind to

trust your voice has value and that you speak up early and often

fill your mind with positive thoughts and not those that limit you, make you afraid to take risks or believe that you are not enough

continue to be kind and brave rather than pretty and perfect

live every day building toward a full and bold vision of a life you deserve, pulled by passion, love and community, not guilt

I believe this version of you is possible.

My personal vision is that my daughter, your daughter, the world's daughters have this opportunity. As Kamala Harris, the first Black and South Asian female vice president of the United States, said in November 2020, "While I may be the first woman in this office, I will not be the last—because every little girl watching tonight sees that this is a country of possibilities."

My personal vision is to ensure that you feel this way too, that we all do. And I believe it's possible. Can you imagine how things could change if we worked toward that world together? No doubt, no patriarchy, no perfectionism. No bias, no barriers, no stereotypes. No limits, no tunnel vision, no rumination. No excuses, no exception. Possibility for everyone.

That's what drives me to keep working with aspiring and experienced leaders like you. It's that desire to keep affirming ourselves, pressing our organizations and its leaders and questioning our societies and cultures so that the next generation of women can pursue their careers without as many hurdles.

Do you share these aspirations for a better world? Do you believe it's possible for yourself and others?

We are wired for possibility

I know it doesn't always feel like it, but we are wired for possibility. When we believe in something, we behave in different ways.

I was reminded of this one sunny spring morning as I set out for a walk along a lake. It was April, that tricky time of year in Canada. Mother Nature decides whether it will be cold, cool, warm or hot. One year you can be shoveling snow and the next you can get a sunburn. All week, the weather people were promising a high of 15 degrees Celsius (59 degrees Fahrenheit, you're welcome), which would have been a welcome relief after a long, cold, snowy winter. People weren't just eager for it; they were desperate for it. It was a topic of conversation all week.

But when I left the house that morning at 8:30 a.m., it was just 4 degrees. I was disappointed because I knew there was no way it was going to warm up to the promised high by midday. I'm not a pessimist; it's just much windier and colder when you're by the lake like I am. I sighed and reached for my winter coat and set out for my walk. *Maybe tomorrow will be warmer*, I thought.

As I got closer to the boardwalk that lines the lake, I had to look twice. There were hundreds of people everywhere. Even though the temperature was the same as the weekend prior, there were infinitely more people out. There were bikes, scooters and kids playing everywhere. Runners donned shorts for the first time that season. It was still cold, but we acted like it was warm because there was a possibility that it might be. You could feel the energy in the air. It was officially spring according to the calendar, and people were acting like it even though it was only 4 degrees. There was a possibility that it could happen, and they made it so.

I believe that you can create your world as you dream it to be. I know it's within your reach to feel empowered and to shape your life and your career to be full of possibilities. I know because I've heard the stories of those who have done it, who are doing it. You'll know you're on the right track when you feel lighter and stronger at the same time. Where you stop caring what others think and start living your life, your career, your vision. It's possible.

Reframe your story

Humans have patterns of thoughts and behaviors. We tell ourselves stories that reinforce our beliefs and our actions. You have ways of thinking that have become entrenched within you, stories that have become your defaults. Sometimes these stories help you and sometimes they get in the way of your success. As you read each chapter, I bet you noticed some common stories that get in the way for you.

What should you do now? Start small and determine one shift you'd like to make. There may be many swirling around in your brain after reading the chapters and capturing the from-to reframing statements. Choose one reframe that will give you the strongest forward momentum right now. Which reframe will you decide to focus on today?

Take five minutes now to capture your reframe and next steps.

My reframe:

_____

_____

_____

_____

_____

My two to three actions to take:

_____

_____

_____

_____

_____

_____

_____

My upcoming practice opportunities:

_____

_____

_____

_____

_____

_____

Find opportunities in your everyday routines to practice shifting your mindset and the stories you tell yourself. Try some tips, techniques and strategies you've learned here and elsewhere. Engage a feedback partner and you'll make faster movement. Then move to another reframe. Soon you will not only feel more confident, but also others will notice these subtle shifts in you.

Uncovering and discovering your stories is an ongoing endeavor. Try journaling to get out your thoughts and revisit the entries with an eye to discovering default patterns or assumptions that can be reframed. Share your stories with trusted friends, a coach or engage in a retreat. Sharing our stories with the support of objective and empathetic ears makes reframing them easier.

This is the way you change the stories for yourself. Your stories inform your actions, and your actions reinforce your stories. You can make the cycle more positive. Now let's look at how we create positive stories more broadly.

Our collective opportunity is now

Whether you like it or not, you are part of a movement today. We are at a point in history when a number of cultural, societal and political forces are converging to the benefit of women everywhere. Protests and movements in the last few years have gained momentum and visibility in a way we haven't seen since the 1960s and 1970s when women's liberation burst into the public consciousness.

You cannot open a single paper, channel or media feed without seeing coverage on women's advancement—whether it's the number of women in the executive ranks or on boards, evolution of family supportive policies, equal pay, safety and respect in the workplace and at home, or our rights to go to school, drive a car or bicycle, walk safely alone at night or attend a football match. While there has been some tremendous movement in the fight for female advancement, it is not fast enough. We will celebrate small and big wins and keep going.

The sad reality is that many women feel powerless to make change. It often feels too big to comprehend. Too heavy and entrenched a stone to move.

A woman came up to me after I gave a speech to her company in celebration of International Women's Day. She was visibly irritated. She grappled with the sheer enormity of the gender equality problem. How on earth can we as individuals solve a challenge that is so far reaching and pervasive? How can we impact entire cultures and societies? How can we change public policy and organizational rules?

She then described to me how she tries to raise her young children with gender progressive views. She reminds her son, for example, that pink is not a color only for girls, and that her daughter can look in any toy aisle she pleases—not just at the toys designated for girls. They both have to help out around the home and are encouraged to be rough and tumble outside. But the world around us, she argues, constantly reinforces what is socially acceptable for a boy versus a girl. "It just doesn't seem like enough. How can individuals really make any difference?" she asked.

And that's when I reminded that frustrated woman to keep on going. She was already watching for defaults and unhelpful stories. She was helping to change patterns of thinking in others. I congratulated her on recognizing those moments with her own children to create a more progressive world. You must keep it up, I urged her. We must keep the conversation going and spur action. If we do nothing, things will either remain the same or get worse. We can't sit back and hope that things will magically change.

We cannot wait for the world around us to evolve before we take action. Each of us can make movement in our own way. As Malala Yousafzai, an activist for female education and the youngest Nobel Prize laureate, eloquently said, "When the whole world is silent, even one voice becomes powerful." You don't have to do the same things Yousafzai has done; don't get paralyzed by believing you must have near the same impact. Every small act, every small conversation with yourself and others makes an impact on embracing a new story.

Because you are living in this time, you are part of the historical conversation on women's rights, on double binds, on stereotypes, on our place in this world. What role do you want to play? Active or passive, big or small, local or global. It doesn't matter. But you are living in a defining moment in history. You're here whether you like it or not. Will you help change the story for yourself and for others?

Don't rely on the next generation; fortify them and their future

A man of the Boomer generation approached me after I gave a keynote speech on women's advancement. I'm mid Gen X and he looked late Boomer so I was curious to hear what he wanted to say. We talked about the state of gender equality and the progress achieved (or lack thereof). He said to me, "Tammy, we have been shaped through tens of thousands of years, right back to the caveman era. Things will not change overnight and they will not change as quickly as we want them to. But this younger generation coming up, they're different. It will be different with them."

That's a common sentiment I hear when I work with organizations and their leaders on creating a diverse and inclusive culture: this promise that the youth will provide a better future. When we get rid of the old guard, things will change. But are the up-and-coming generations really going to shift things so dramatically? Are they being raised to think so differently? I'm not so sure, because they're learning from us.

Sure, today's younger generations are growing up in a more global society, surrounded with greater diversity and exposed to a broader definition of what constitutes family. They have greater concern for our climate and are shaping expectations for more balanced work lives. But when it comes to gender roles and hardwired thinking, have things really changed that much?

Girls are still discouraged or embarrassed to pursue STEMM. Teenage boys have more leisure time to play sports, game or watch TV, while girls spend more time with homework, grooming, housework and errands.

While I agree with the man's caveman comment in theory—that change won't happen as quickly as we want—I reject that we should simply wait to evolve into a better future. I refuse to pin our hopes on future generations to figure it out. Without our guidance, the youth of today will be no further ahead than we are. Caveman behavior is alive and well all around us. And not just with grownups in the boardroom or in politics but on the playground too.

"Real change,
enduring change,
happens one
step at a time."

RUTH BADER GINSBURG

Take this example. In a sandwich shop, I overheard two young boys talking trivia. They argued over who was the first person to take flight. One boy said Amelia Earhart and the other mocked his answer saying, "She was the first *woman* but not the first to fly. As if! She's a chick." Some may view this as playful banter between boys. I call it reinforcement of gender stereotypes.

These conversations are everywhere if you listen for them. When I told this story during a speech, a woman came up to me after and said, "Tammy, I have two young boys. How do I raise them to make space for girls? I don't want to squash their confidence. It's good for them to be confident."

Of course, you don't want to squash their confidence; it is a good thing, I told her. Are you teaching them about the fine line between confidence and arrogance? Can they understand the difference between self-assurance and conceit? Can they decipher when to be bold and when to be modest? Teach them about empathy, I implored. Teach them about how their words and behaviors impact others. Teach them to use their confidence to build others up, not tear them down. Teach them that vulnerability is not a weakness. Teach them to be inclusive. "I have never thought about it that way," she said. "You have given me a lot to think about."

Dr. Alice Eagly is a professor of psychology and of management and organizations at Northwestern University. She is often quoted in research papers for her expertise on female leadership and stereotypes. She reminds us that "stereotypes change when people get new observations. They form because of what people experience in daily life, what people see."

I was reminded of this acutely as I worked with a manufacturing client who was beginning their diversity and inclusion journey. I gave a keynote to their top one hundred leaders on the role they play in shaping the culture of their organization. I reminded them of the power they wielded to shape the trajectory of all their people. After the keynote, the leaders were split into groups to determine ways to move the organization forward and specifically to create more inclusiveness and opportunities for women.

I needed a number of facilitators to lead the breakout groups. I was pleasantly surprised that two of my male colleagues passionately volunteered to be part of the team. One in particular said he had a personal connection to the topic of removing biases and stereotypes, specifically with and for women. As I listened to him share his story with this organization's leaders, I understood why.

Growing up, he was close friends with a neighborhood girl. They were inseparable as kids. The girl always said she wanted to be a doctor, and she didn't waver from that aspiration as she grew older. Whenever she voiced her dream, my colleague would say, "You mean a nurse." "A doctor!" she would repeatedly correct him, to which he repeatedly corrected her back.

That young girl did grow up to be a doctor. And my colleague was so glad. He explained that as a boy he was quite ill and spent a lot of time in hospitals. He noticed a pattern during his many nights in his hospital bed. Doctors were men and nurses were women. That's what he observed during his long stay, so that's how it must be.

This experience had a lasting impact on him and has shaped his approach to leadership as an adult. Upon reflection, my colleague regrets not talking to anyone about his observations. He didn't question his assumptions; he accepted it as his default frame of reference. He can't imagine the biases his friend must have experienced throughout her journey to become a doctor. She probably continues to face challenges in a field that is still male dominated. He laments that he was the first to doubt her or may have made her doubt her dream. He is invested now as a leader himself and as a coach to help others see what defaults, biases or frames of reference are getting in the way for them and the people around them. His early experience made him passionate about helping others succeed and in helping organizations realize how they're standing in the way of their employees feeling that they matter, that the future they envision is possible.

My colleague learned to tell himself a new story by challenging his early entrenched observations. Together we can change the stories we tell ourselves and each other.

One story can make all
the difference (even a math story)

By the time I get to work with my clients, they are advanced in their careers—some at the top of their game. Yet the issue of unhelpful, self-limiting stories continues to be a challenge. We can change this cycle earlier on. What if we could see and seize these moments in girls in their formative years?

I did just that when my daughter bemoaned an upcoming test in math, her least favorite subject. As we got our coats on to rush out the door, I asked how she was feeling about the test that morning. She promptly launched into a huff. "I hate math. I'm not good at it and I know I'm going to fail." Her hands went up into the air, her face fell, and her voice rose a few octaves. She was a veritable physical and emotional mess in the making.

Because I had seen her practicing her math questions, I knew her fear of failing this test was unlikely to be realized. However, her reaction made me remember with dread the studies I had read about girls going into math tests thinking they were terrible, then doing worse than those who were told and thought they were good at it. I took a deep breath and stopped zipping up my coat. This was one of those important moments to change the story she was telling herself. If I was ten minutes late for my first meeting, it would be worth it in the grand scheme of things.

I took my daughter's hand and said, "Let's chat for a minute." I started with "Did you know that studies have shown that when girls go into math tests thinking they'll fail, they actually do worse?" To which she responded with an eye roll and sigh. My husband gave a supportive "Hey, listen to Mom; she knows about this stuff." I continued to explain that it was important for her to feel confident that she had prepared herself and that she could do well. We talked about the practice tests she already successfully completed. I told her I didn't expect her to love math like she did other subjects, but that I wanted her to believe she could do well with the right effort. (Thank you, Dr. Carol Dweck, for your book *Mindset*, which has literally changed my life and how I parent.) I ended by explaining that studies have shown that girls did better on tests when they believed in themselves.

"Weird," she said.

"Could you try that today?" I asked.

Later my daughter came to me and said, "Hey Mom, I felt confident with my math test and I think I answered almost all the questions right, but the girl who sits next to me was complaining and said, 'I don't know how to do this. I hate math! I'm going to fail.'"

"What did you say to her?"

"I told her she should believe in herself."

ACKNOWLEDGMENTS

HA. I DID IT. I actually made it to the end. Who would have thought? Well, luckily a lot of people knew I could and spurred me on when I doubted it myself. And I want to thank them here.

To all the women I've relished taking through grueling workshops, mentored or who reached out to chat after a keynote or reading an article—thank you for sharing your stories, being open with your struggles and being brave enough to try new things. Hearing about your transformations, your breakthrough conversations and how you changed the stories you tell yourself is what keeps me doing this rewarding and important work. Nothing brings a greater smile to my face than seeing your promotions pop up on LinkedIn. Keep on keepin' on.

To my mentors David, Neville, Janet, Ren and Lucy. You may know it, or you may not, but conversations with you over the years have made me stronger and wiser. I guess now you know, so thanks a bunch. To Vince and Liane who created the ridiculous expectation that a book could be written in four months—what the hell? You didn't waver in your belief that I had it in me. And if you did, I appreciate you not letting me know. Liane, many thanks for the guidance, the brainstorming, the picking up and dusting off and reminding me that I had important messages to share with the world.

To the Page Two team who worked with me, thank you for your expertise, wisdom and support. You make the arduous task of writing a book infinitely easier not only because of your knowledge but also because you're fun and easy to work with. Thank you for making me sound smart, look good and able to get the book in as many readers' hands as possible. Jesse and Amanda—you sure do know how to buoy a person's heart. Thank you for your personal enthusiasm for my message, for sharing how my book made you think differently (even the early crappy drafts) and for your eagerness to share the book with people in your own lives.

To my tribe of women who are always there to listen, to share, to support, to bitch and to celebrate: Lara, Annette, Tithie, Krista, Ang, Jessica, Liane D, Ivy, Sheila, Lisa, Tess, Razia, Sandra, Liane T, Kirsten—we shine, and we soar, together. To Carla and Claudine who helped raise my daughter into the kind, clever and empathetic person she is today. You made the time away from home infinitely easier. Your strength, intelligence, drive and goodness make you role models for any child or executive alike.

To my family—Mom, Dad, Curtis and Lisa—who made it possible for me to take big risks early on. You supported my dreams, and my wallet, so that I could explore the world, learn with the best and eventually make my own way. To my godmother Cheryl who lives the farthest away but felt closest in my heart when I sought to dream, to travel and to explore what was possible.

To my husband, Thomas, an equal partner and the kindest man I've ever known. You took a step back when I wanted to step forward; you stood beside me when I wanted to change and you stood in front when I needed a wall to lean on.

To my Ava. Sorry if being in this book embarrasses you and for the stress that comes with being a petri dish in the lab of women's leadership we call home. I know you'll get over it when you're older because you'll realize then that I did it all for you. I push you because I want you to believe in yourself. I question you because I want you to stand up for yourself with conviction. And I think one day you just might like trading inspirational quotes and meditating with me.

NOTES

Introduction: You Need New Stories

on Equal Pay Day . . . Equal Pay Day raises awareness of the gender pay gap. The day, which differs from year to year, symbolizes how far into the year the average woman must work to earn what the average man earned in the entire previous year (regardless of experience or job type).

you will never completely erase these negative voices . . . Emily Nagoski and Amelia Nagoski, *Burnout: The Secret to Unlocking the Stress Cycle* (New York: Ballantine Books, 2020).

best to focus on structural issues or the tactical DIY strategies . . . Jae Yun Kim, Gráinne M. Fitzsimons and Aaron C. Kay, "Lean In Messages Increase Attributions of Women's Responsibility for Gender Inequality," *Journal of Personality and Social Psychology* 115, no. 6 (2018): 974–1001, doi.org/10.1037/pspa0000129.

1: Believe It's Possible

sustainable pipeline of female CEOs . . . Jane Edison Stevenson and Evelyn Orr, "We Interviewed 57 Female CEOs to Find Out How More Women Can Get to the Top," *Harvard Business Review*, November 8, 2017, hbr.org/2017/11/we-interviewed -57-female-ceos-to-find-out-how-more-women-can-get-to-the-top.

The 2015 KPMG Women's Leadership Study . . . KPMG Women's Leadership Study, *Moving Women Forward into Leadership Roles*, 2015, home.kpmg/content/dam/kpmg/ ph/pdf/ThoughtLeadershipPublications/KPMGWomensLeadershipStudy.pdf.

The 2019 KPMG Women's Leadership Study . . . KPMG Women's Leadership Study, *Risk, Resilience, Reward*, 2019, info.kpmg.us/content/dam/info/en/news-perspectives/ pdf/2019/KPMG_Womens_Leadership_Study.pdf.

Leadership self-efficacy refers to . . . Michael McCormick, Jesús Tanguma and Anita Sohn López-Forment, "Extending Self-Efficacy Theory to Leadership: A Review and Empirical Test," *Journal of Leadership Education* 1, no. 2 (2002): 34–49, doi.org/ 10.12806/V1/I2/TF1.

whether leadership self-efficacy could be increased... Carol Isaac, Anna Kaatz, Barbara
   Lee and Molly Carnes, "An Educational Intervention Designed to Increase Wom-
   en's Leadership Self-Efficacy," CBE Life Sciences Education 11, no. 3 (Fall 2012):
   201–332, doi.org/10.1187/cbe.12-02-0022.
global phenomenon called "think manager, think male"... Virginia E. Schein and Marilyn
   J. Davidson, "Think Manager, Think Male," Management Development Review 6,
   no. 3 (1993), doi.org/10.1108/EUM0000000000738.
We need to have leaders... Tomas Chamorro-Premuzic as quoted in Janice Gassam
   Asare, "Why So Many Unqualified and Incompetent Men Continue to Rise," Forbes,
   November 5, 2019, forbes.com/sites/janicegassam/2019/11/05/why-so-many
   -unqualified-and-incompetent-men-continue-to-rise/?sh=c89c2b46d26e.
Research shows that women tend to score higher... Jack Zenger and Joseph Folk-
   man, "Research: Women Score Higher Than Men in Most Leadership Skills,"
   Harvard Business Review, June 25, 2019, hbr.org/2019/06/research-women
   -score-higher-than-men-in-most-leadership-skills.
Women-owned companies are also shown to have higher returns... Allyson Kapin, "10
   Stats That Build the Case for Investing in Women-Led Startups," Forbes, January
   28, 2019, forbes.com/sites/allysonkapin/2019/01/28/10-stats-that-build-the
   -case-for-investing-in-women-led-startups.
more value-creating strategies... Corinne Post, Boris Lokshin and Christophe Boone,
   "Research: Adding Women to the C-Suite Changes How Companies Think," Harvard Business Review, April 6, 2021, hbr.org/2021/04/research-adding-women
   -to-the-c-suite-changes-how-companies-think.
We retire with two-thirds the money that men have... Sallie Krawcheck, Own It: The
   Power of Women at Work (New York: Currency, 2017).

2: Look Up, Look Out

experiences of women at all levels of corporations... Working Mother Research Institute and National Association for Female Executives, The Gender Gap at the Top:
   What's Keeping Women from Leading Corporate America?, 2019, workingmother
   .com/sites/workingmother.com/files/attachments/2019/06/women_at_the_top_
   correct_size.pdf.
women still carry the burden of caretaking responsibilities... Sarah Coury, Jess Huang,
   Ankur Kumar, Sara Prince, Alexis Krivkovich and Lareina Yee, Women in the
   Workplace 2020, McKinsey & Company, September 30, 2020, mckinsey.com/
   featured-insights/diversity-and-inclusion/women-in-the-workplace.
Boston Consulting Group (BCG) surveyed 200,000 employees... Katie Abouzahr,
   Matt Krentz, Claire Tracey and Miki Tsusaka, "Dispelling the Myths of the
   Gender 'Ambition Gap,'" Boston Consulting Group (BCG), April 5, 2017, bcg
   .com/publications/2017/people-organization-leadership-change-dispelling
   -the-myths-of-the-gender-ambition-gap.
many studies exploring the hurdles to advancement... Dasie J. Schulz and Chris-
   tine Enslin, "The Female Executive's Perspective on Career Planning and
   Advancement in Organizations: Experiences with Cascading Gender Bias, the
   Double-Bind, and Unwritten Rules to Advancement," SAGE Open 4, no. 4 (2014):
   1–9, doi.org/10.1177/2158244014558040.

the constraining effect of cultural beliefs about gender... Shelley J. Correll, "Constraints into Preferences: Gender, Status, and Emerging Career Aspirations," *American Sociological Review* 69, no. 1 (2004): 93-113, doi.org/10.1177/000312240406900106.

The Hay Group highlighted learning for learning's sake... Ruth Malloy, "Don't Let Your Career 'Just Happen,'" *Harvard Business Review*, September 6, 2013, hbr.org/2013/09/dont-let-your-career-just-happ.

women hold nearly 60 percent of advanced degrees... Dina Gerdeman, "How Gender Stereotypes Kill a Woman's Self-Confidence," Harvard Business School Working Knowledge, February 25, 2019, hbswk.hbs.edu/item/how-gender-stereotypes-less-than-br-greater-than-kill-a-woman-s-less-than-br-greater-than-self-confidence.

an in-depth study of twelve female CEOs... Andromachi Athanasopoulou, Amanda Moss Cowan, Michael Smets and Timothy Morris, "In Interviews, Female CEOs Say They Don't Expect Much Support—at Home or at Work," *Harvard Business Review*, June 15, 2018, hbr.org/2018/06/in-interviews-female-ceos-say-they-dont-expect-much-support-at-home-or-at-work.

engagement and retention of women in the engineering profession... Kathleen R. Buse and Diana Bilimoria, "Personal Vision: Enhancing Work Engagement and the Retention of Women in the Engineering Profession," *Frontiers in Psychology* 5, 1400 (2014), doi.org/10.3389/fpsyg.2014.01400.

associated with lower risk of all-cause mortality... Ann Marie Roepke, Eranda Jayawickreme and Olivia M. Riffle, "Meaning and Health: A Systematic Review," *Applied Research in Quality of Life* 9, no. 4 (2014): 1055-79, doi.org/10.1007/s11482-013-9288-9.

an interesting gender difference found... Rachel Morrison, "What Research Tells Us about Gender Difference in Perceptions of Ability at Work," World Economic Forum, August 14, 2018, weforum.org/agenda/2018/08/gender-differences-at-work-relishing-competence-or-seeking-a-challenge/.

most people don't find their passion at work... John Coleman, "You Don't Find Your Purpose—You Build It," *Harvard Business Review*, October 20, 2017, hbr.org/2017/10/you-dont-find-your-purpose-you-build-it.

3: Do Less Shit

studied thousands of 360 assessments... Herminia Ibarra and Otilia Obodaru, "Women and the Vision Thing," *Harvard Business Review*, January 2009, hbr.org/2009/01/women-and-the-vision-thing.

studies exploring gender differences in delegation... Modupe Akinola, Ashley E. Martin and Katherine W. Phillips, "To Delegate or Not to Delegate: Gender Differences in Affective Associations and Behavioral Responses to Delegation," *Academy of Management Journal* 61, no. 4 (2018): 1467-91, doi.org/10.5465/amj.2016.0662.

women spend five hours per week on office housekeeping tasks... Linda Babcock, Maria Recalde, Lise Vesterlund and Laurie Weingart, "Gender Differences in Accepting and Receiving Requests for Tasks with Low Promotability," *American Economic Review* 107, no. 3 (2017): 714-47, doi.org/10.1257/aer.20141734.

You have to decide what your highest priorities are ... Stephen Covey quoted in Chris McChesney, Jim Huling and Sean Covey, *The 4 Disciplines of Execution: Achieving Your Wildly Important Goals* (New York: Simon & Schuster, 2015), 30.

4: Rule That Meeting

teachers call on boys more ... Soraya Chemaly, "All Teachers Should Be Trained to Overcome Their Hidden Biases," *Time*, February 12, 2015, time.com/3705454/teachers -biases-girls-education.

too aggressive when they do participate ... Lucy Vernasco, "Seven Studies That Prove Mansplaining Exists," *Bitch Media*, July 14, 2014, bitchmedia.org/post/seven-studies -proving-mansplaining-exists.

Women downplay their certainty by using qualifiers ... Deborah Tannen, "The Power of Talk: Who Gets Heard and Why," *Harvard Business Review*, September–October 1995, hbr.org/1995/09/the-power-of-talk-who-gets-heard-and-why.

girls tend to play with a single best friend ... Tannen, "The Power of Talk."

the assertive/aggressive stereotype ... Marguerite Rigoglioso, "Researchers: How Women Can Succeed in the Workplace," Insights by Stanford Business, March 1, 2011, gsb.stanford.edu/insights/researchers-how-women-can-succeed-workplace.

analyzed over two hundred performance reviews from a tech company ... Shelley J. Correll and Caroline Simard, "Research: Vague Feedback Is Holding Women Back," *Harvard Business Review*, April 29, 2016, hbr.org/2016/04/research-vague-feedback -is-holding-women-back.

Women who could read the situation ... Rigoglioso, "Researchers."

multiyear study looked at this dynamic in 236 engineers ... Margarita Mayo, "To Seem Confident, Women Have to Be Seen as Warm," *Harvard Business Review*, July 8, 2016, hbr.org/2016/07/to-seem-confident-women-have-to-be-seen-as-warm.

marriage of warmth and competence is the magical combination ... Amy J.C. Cuddy, Matthew Kohut and John Neffinger, "Connect, Then Lead," *Harvard Business Review*, July–August 2013, hbr.org/2013/07/connect-then-lead.

5: Own It, Flaunt It, Get It

difference in the language that male and female researchers used ... Marc J. Lerchenmueller, Olav Sorenson and Anupam B. Jena, "Gender Differences in How Scientists Present the Importance of Their Research: Observational Study," *BMJ* 367 (2019), doi.org/10.1136/bmj.l6573.

fun survey called the Self-Promotion Gap ... Mighty Forces, Southpaw Insights, Upstream Analysis and Grey Horse Communications, "The Self-Promotion Gap," selfpromotiongap.com/home.

men and women felt discomfort when engaging in self-promotion ... Corinne A. Moss-Racusin and Laurie A. Rudman, "Disruptions in Women's Self-Promotion: The Backlash Avoidance Model," *Psychology of Women Quarterly* 34, no. 2 (2010): 186–202, doi.org/10.1111/j.1471-6402.2010.01561.x.

studied the area of self-promotion and modesty ... Marie-Hélène Budworth and Sara L. Mann, "Becoming a Leader: The Challenge of Modesty for Women," *Journal of Management Development* 29, no. 2 (2010): 177–86, doi.org/10.1108/026217 11011019314.

Self-advocacy is learning how to speak up for yourself... "Best Practices in Self-Advocacy Skill Building," Center for Parent Information & Resources, updated March 2019, parentcenterhub.org/priority-selfadvocacy.

6: Think *Who* before *Do*

networking, informal decision-making and organizational politics... Kathryn Heath, Jill Flynn and Mary Davis Holt, "Women, Find Your Voice," *Harvard Business Review*, June 2014, hbr.org/2014/06/women-find-your-voice.

often referred to as organizational politics... "What Is Organizational Politics?" Reference .com, last updated April 7, 2020, reference.com/business-finance/organizational -politics-df167f40b547fd36.

women had less overlap in their networks than men... Herminia Ibarra, "Why Strategic Networking Is Harder for Women," World Economic Forum, April 7, 2016, weforum .org/agenda/2016/04/why-strategic-networking-is-harder-for-women/.

She found that men tend to seek friendship... Monica M. Stallings, "Reaching Up: The Influence of Gender, Status, and Relationship Type on Men's and Women's Network Preferences," PhD dissertation (University of Pennsylvania), Publicly Accessible Penn Dissertations 144 (2010), repository.upenn.edu/edissertations/ 144.

the more we differ from key stakeholders... Ibarra, "Why Strategic Networking Is Harder for Women."

women felt morally conflicted about leveraging their network... Elena Greguletz, Marjo-Riitta Diehl and Karin Kreutzer, "Why Women Build Less Effective Networks Than Men: The Role of Structural Exclusion and Personal Hesitation," *Human Relations* 72, no. 7 (2019): 1234–61, doi.org/10.1177/0018726718804303.

most people are focused on performance currency instead of relationship currency... Carla A. Harris, *Strategize to Win: The New Way to Start Out, Step Up, or Start Over in Your Career* (New York: Hudson Street Press, 2014).

operational, personal and strategic... Herminia Ibarra and Mark Lee Hunter, "How Leaders Create and Use Networks," *Harvard Business Review*, January 2007, hbr.org/ 2007/01/how-leaders-create-and-use-networks.

researched organizational politics for over two decades... Gerald R. Ferris, Pamela L. Perrewé, B. Parker Ellen III, Charn P. McAllister and Darren C. Treadway, *Political Skill at Work: How to Influence, Motivate, and Win Support* (New York: Mobius, 2020).

differences between men and women when it comes to office politics... Kathryn Heath, Jill Flynn, Mary Davis Holt and Diana Faison, *The Influence Effect: A New Path to Power for Women Leaders* (San Francisco, CA: Berrett-Koehler, 2017).

women can become better at politics if they redefine it... Harvey Schachter, "How Women Can Improve at Office Politics," *Globe and Mail*, January 18, 2012, theglobeandmail.com/report-on-business/careers/management/how-women -can-improve-at-office-politics/article37616931.

Being politically savvy can even lead to less stress... Pamela L. Perrewé, Gerald R. Ferris, Dwight D. Frink and William P. Anthony, "Political Skill: An Antidote for Workplace Stressors," *The Academy of Management Executive* 14, no. 3 (2000): 115–23, doi.org/10.5465/ame.2000.4468071.

7: Lighten Up, Brain

women suffer higher levels of anxiety than men... Olivia Remes, "Women Are Far More Anxious Than Men—Here's the Science," *The Conversation*, June 10, 2016, theconversation.com/women-are-far-more-anxious-than-men-heres-the -science-60458.

one important component: self-compassion... See the abundant research by Dr. Kristin Neff on her website: self-compassion.org/the-research.

pull between being the ideal worker and the ideal mother... Caitlyn Collins, *Making Motherhood Work: How Women Manage Careers and Caregiving* (Princeton, NJ: Princeton University Press, 2019).

most people think of productivity as how fast they can get everything done... Alice Boyes, "Don't Let Perfection Be the Enemy of Productivity," *Harvard Business Review*, March 3, 2020, hbr.org/2020/03/dont-let-perfection-be-the-enemy -of-productivity.

women in particular are prone to feelings of guilt... Linda Torstveit, Stefan Sütterlin and Ricardo Gregorio Lugo, "Empathy, Guilt Proneness, and Gender: Relative Contributions to Prosocial Behaviour," *Europe's Journal of Psychology* 12, no. 2 (2016): 260–70, doi.org/10.5964/ejop.v12i2.1097.

Guilt is defined as an emotion... Susan Krauss Whitbourne, "The Definitive Guide to Guilt: Five Types of Guilt and How You Can Cope with Each," *Psychology Today*, August 11, 2012, psychologytoday.com/us/blog/fulfillment-any-age/201208/ the-definitive-guide-guilt.

a lesson Magdalena Yesil learned the hard way... Julian Guthrie, *Alpha Girls: The Women Upstarts Who Took On Silicon Valley's Male Culture and Made the Deals of a Lifetime* (New York: Currency, 2019).

the human giver syndrome... Kate Manne, *Down Girl: The Logic of Misogyny* (Oxford: Oxford University Press, 2017).

women engage in rumination more than men... Daniel P. Johnson and Mark A. Whisman, "Gender Differences in Rumination: A Meta-Analysis," *Personality and Individual Differences* 55, no. 4 (2013): 367–74, doi.org/10.1016/j.paid.2013 .03.019.

Psychologists refer to this phenomenon as maternal gatekeeping... Elissa Strauss, "Maternal Gatekeeping: Why Moms Don't Let Dads Help," CNN Health, December 6, 2017, cnn.com/2017/12/06/health/maternal-gatekeeping-strauss.

Having gratitude is critical to our well-being... Robert Emmons, "Why Gratitude Is Good," *Greater Good Magazine*, November 16, 2010, greatergood.berkeley.edu/ article/item/why_gratitude_is_good.

For gratitude to have the best impact... Nagoski and Nagoski, *Burnout*.

Jane Fraser, the first female CEO of a major Wall Street bank... Anne Sraders, "This Advice Helped Incoming Citigroup CEO Jane Fraser through a Pivotal Time in Her Career," *Fortune*, September 30, 2020, fortune.com/2020/09/30/citigroup -ceo-jane-fraser-career-advice-mpw-summit.

daughters of working mothers grew up to be more successful... Kathleen L. McGinn, Mayra Ruiz Castro and Elizabeth Long Lingo, "Learning from Mum: Cross-National Evidence Linking Maternal Employment and Adult Children's Outcomes," *Work, Employment and Society* 33, no. 3 (2019): 374–400, doi.org/10.1177/ 0950017018760167.

reduce rumination and increase mental health . . . Gregory N. Bratman et al., "Affective Benefits of Nature Contact: The Role of Rumination," *Frontiers in Psychology* 12 (2021), doi.org/10.3389/fpsyg.2021.643866.

A sign of wisdom is not believing everything you think . . . Adam Grant (@AdamMGrant), "A sign of wisdom is not believing everything you think," Twitter, January 29, 2020, 10:11 a.m., twitter.com/AdamMGrant/status/1222537799288655873.

Conclusion: Our New Stories

When the whole world is silent . . . Brian MacQuarrie, "Malala Yousafzai Addresses Harvard Audience," *Boston Globe*, September 27, 2013, bostonglobe.com/metro/2013/ 09/27/malala-yousafzai-pakistani-teen-shot-taliban-tells-harvard-audience-that -education-right-for-all/6cZBanoM4J3cAnmRZLfUmI/story.html.

Teenage boys have more leisure time . . . Gretchen Livingston, "The Way U.S. Teens Spend Their Time Is Changing, but Differences between Boys and Girls Persist," Pew Research Center, February 20, 2019, pewresearch.org/fact-tank/2019/02/20/ the-way-u-s-teens-spend-their-time-is-changing-but-differences-between-boys -and-girls-persist.

stereotypes change when people get new observations . . . Alice Eagly as quoted in Alia E. Dastagir, "Women Are Now Seen as Equally Intelligent as Men, Study Finds," *USA Today*, July 18, 2019, usatoday.com/story/news/nation/2019/07/18/differences -between-men-and-women-most-now-say-intelligence-equal/1767610001.

studies I had read about girls going into math tests . . . Paul R. Jones, "Reducing the Impact of Stereotype Threat on Women's Math Performance: Are Two Strategies Better Than One?" *Electronic Journal of Research in Educational Psychology* 9, no. 2 (2011): 587–616, pubmed.ncbi.nlm.nih.gov/22545058/.

Thank you, Dr. Carol Dweck . . . Carol S. Dweck, *Mindset: The New Psychology of Success* (New York: Ballantine, 2006).

INDEX

ABOUT THE AUTHOR

David Leyes

TAMMY HEERMANN is an award-winning leadership expert sought out by some of the world's top companies for her programs that accelerate women's advancement. For over twenty years, she has helped change thousands of mindsets on what it takes to lead, both self and others. While having impact in the C-suite, nothing makes her happier than pushing up-and-coming leaders to break through organizational and self-imposed barriers to reach their potential. Tammy transforms her audiences with alternating moments of humor and heartache as she shares stories of her own journey from senior consultant to senior vice president. She is a perennial mentor with Women in Communications and Technology and is also addicted to the Peloton, Pilates and perogies. She lives in Toronto with her husband and daughter.

TammyHeermann.com

Inspire, skill up and accelerate the women in your organization

Maybe your organization is already working on diversity initiatives, or maybe you wish it was doing more. Tap into the expertise of an award-winning leadership pro with a passion for advancing women. Here's how I can help.

Inspire

Books for everyone: Buy copies of the book to support your development programs, resource groups or diversity and inclusion initiatives. Contact me about bulk discounts for large groups.

Keynotes: Experience the art of storytelling, the credibility of research-based insights and the practicality of strategies you can use the minute the presentation is over. Ideal for networking events, management retreats and other forums where there is a need to challenge beliefs, inspire action and provide pragmatic ways to advance women in leadership.

Skill up

Workshops: Two hours or two days, in person or virtual, benefit from content that feels like it was custom designed for you. Engage in experiential workshops that challenge mindsets, build skills and create a community of network relationships for the long term. Inquire about workshops for women and for the people managers and executive leaders who are critical support for women's advancement.

Accelerate

High-potential programs: Invest in small cohorts to accelerate and advance your female pipeline with integrated development programs that transform your people and your culture.

Let's chat and figure out how we can work together to change the stories for all of us.

tammy@tammyheermann.com
TammyHeermann.com
LI TammyHeermann

Manufactured by Amazon.ca
Bolton, ON